if ~~one~~ I am is to lead a meaningful
life in the digital age and
prevent death by internet penetration
I will have to take control
and select those images —
moving and still, I want to
view, it's a challenge to
forgo the incessant looking
at the cell phone, I've limited
my time to 2 hours a day.

ONE-WAY STREET

ONE-WAY STREET

WALTER BENJAMIN

TRANSLATED BY
Edmund Jephcott

EDITED AND WITH
AN INTRODUCTION BY
Michael W. Jennings

PREFACE BY
Greil Marcus

The Belknap Press *of* Harvard University Press
Cambridge, Massachusetts • London, England
2016

Third printing

Library of Congress Cataloging-in-Publication Data

Names: Benjamin, Walter, 1892–1940, author. | Jephcott, E. F. N.,
    translator. | Jennings, Michael William, editor, writer of introduction. |
    Marcus, Greil, writer of preface.
Title: One-way street / Walter Benjamin ; translated by Edmund
    Jephcott; edited and with an introduction by Michael W. Jennings;
    preface by Greil Marcus.
Other titles: Einbahnstrasse. English
Description: Cambridge, Massachusetts : The Belknap Press of Harvard
    University Press, 2016. | Translated from the German. | "One-Way
    Street? originally appeared in English in Reflections by Walter
    Benjamin." | Includes bibliographical references and index.
Identifiers: LCCN 2015039382 | ISBN 9780674052291 (alk. paper)
Subjects: LCSH: Aphorisms and apothegms. | Epigrams. | Philosophy,
    German—20th century.
Classification: LCC PN6283 .B413 2016 | DDC 838/.91209—dc23
    LC record available at http://lccn.loc.gov/2015039382

In Memoriam

MIRIAM BRATU HANSEN

1949–2011

CONTENTS

PREFACE

One day in 1924, a German man in his early thirties steps into a European street. Businesses, shops, signs, public announcements: in the two years that it takes him to reach the end of the street, he notes everything that catches his eye, until the outlines of a city come into view.

Filling Station
Breakfast Room
Number 113
For Men
Standard Clock
Come Back! All Is Forgiven!
Manorially Furnished Ten-Room Apartment
Chinese Curios
Gloves
Mexican Embassy
To the Public: Please Protect and Preserve These
    New Plantings
Construction Site
Ministry of the Interior
Flag . . .
    . . . at Half-Mast
Imperial Panorama
Underground Works

Coiffeur for Easily Embarrassed Ladies
Caution: Steps
Attested Auditor of Books
Teaching Aid
Germans, Drink German Beer!
Post No Bills
Number 13
Ordnance
First Aid
Interior Decoration
Stationers
Fancy Goods
Enlargements
Antiques
Watchmaker and Jeweler
Arc Lamp
Loggia
Lost-and-Found Office
Stand for Not More than Three Cabs
Monument to a Warrior
Fire Alarm
Travel Souvenirs
Optician
Toys
Polyclinic
These Spaces for Rent
Office Equipment
Mixed Cargo: Shipping and Packing
Closed for Alterations

Stamp Shop
Si Parla Italiano
Technical Aid
Hardware
Tax Advice
Legal Protection for the Needy
Doctor's Night-Bell
Madame Ariane: Second Courtyard on the Left
Costume Wardrobe
Betting Office
Stand-Up Beer Hall
No Vagrants!
To the Planetarium

At the same time, in Paris, a man in his mid-twenties enters the Passage de l'Opéra, and, as if sighting the first man's itinerary from across their borders in advance, subsumes his long list down to essentials—"For Men," "Coiffeur for Easily Embarrassed Ladies," and "Stamp Shop"—and catches them all, catches all of life, in a single glimpse.

> Two hairdressers follow the stamp dealer in single file, the first a ladies' hairdresser, the second a *Salon* for Gentlemen. The specializations involved in your functions as hairdressers to the two sexes are by no means lacking in pungency. The laws of the world are inscribed in the letters across your shop fronts.[1]

1. Louis Aragon, *Paris Peasant* (1926), trans. Simon Watson Taylor (Boston: Exact Change, 1994), 38.

A few years after that, in 1930, a Berlin filmmaker cuts hundreds of street sounds—machines starting up, men talking, policemen blowing whistles, children asking questions, doors closing, bells gonging, women singing, pianos playing, with whistling, percussion, or cuckoo clock noises framing it all—into a rhythmic eleven-minute movie without images (it may have been screened as such in a theater), a radio play in which, from then to now, any inhabitant of any industrialized nation could instantly find a place.

Almost fifteen years later, in 1944, a German refugee from the Third Reich, living in Los Angeles, drawn like the first man to a philosophy of names and phrases, begins another map, using philosophical fortune cookies instead of commercial shingles.

> Articles may not be exchanged
> Baby with the bath-water
> Plurale tantum
> Tough Baby
> To them shall no thoughts be turned
> English spoken
> On parle français
> Paysage
> Dwarf fruit
> Pro domo nostra
> Cat out of the bag
> Savages are not more noble
> Out of the firing-line
> Johnny-Head-in-Air

Back to culture
The Health unto Death
This side of the pleasure principle
Invitation to the dance
Ego is Id
Always speak of it, never think of it
Inside and outside
Freedom of thought
Unfair intimidation

Just short of ten years after that, again in Paris, a twenty-year-old, a believer in something he and his fellows call psychogeography, looks at the city as if to leap off of the infinity marked by the first man's last sighting and the prolegomenon to all future cataloging of commercial establishments in the second man's last sentence, listing the most suggestive street names the city has given up.

Bains-Douches des Patriarches
Machines à trancher les viandes
Zoo Notre-Dame
Pharmacie des Sports
Alimentation des Martyrs
Béton translucide
Scierie Main-d'or
Centre de recuperation fonctionnelle
Ambulance Saint-Anne
Cinquième avenue café
Rue des Volontaires Prolongée
Pension de famille dans le jardin

— - a prefatory discussion; that which is said beforehand.

Hôtel des Etrangers
Rue Sauvage

Et la piscine de la rue des Fillettes. Et le com-
missariat de police de la rue du Rendez-vous. La
clinique medico-chirurgicale et le bureau de place-
ment gratuity du quai des Orfèvres. Les fleurs
artificielles de la rue du Soleil. L'hôtel des Caves
du Château, le bar de l'Océan et le café du Va et
Vient. L'hôtel de l'Epoque.

Like others before them and after (Thomas De Quincey's
explorations of London in *Confessions of an English Opium-
Eater* in 1821, Ed Ruscha with his photo-book *Every Building
on the Sunset Strip* in 1966, Laura Oldfield Ford with her
excavations of a ruined London hidden in plain sight in her
zine *Savage Messiah* from 2006 to 2009), these five—Walter
Benjamin, with *One-Way Street*, written between 1924
and 1926 and published in 1928; Louis Aragon, with "The
Passage de l'Opéra," written in 1924 and published as the
first chapter of his *Paysan de Paris* in 1926; Walter Ruttmann, with *Weekend*, "recorded as arbitrary and intentional
elements on the soundtrack of an optical sound film"[2] and
broadcast it in Berlin in June 1930; Theodor Adorno, with
the first part of what would be published in 1951 as *Minima
Moralia*; and Ivan Chtcheglov, under the name Gilles Ivain,
with "Formulary for a New Urbanism," written in 1953 and

2. Barbara Schäfer, notes to *Walter Ruttmann Weekend Remix*, Interme-
dium rec. 003, 2000, compact disc.

published in the first number of the journal *Internationale situationniste* in 1958—were attempting, after the First World War or during and after the Second, to define the peculiar nature of the modern in their century, to capture what was singular about what they would have seen as their shared place and time.

The modern was not necessarily the new: all were aware of what Benjamin called "the revolutionary energies that appear in the 'outmoded.'" Those energies (in "the first iron constructions, the first factory buildings, the earliest photos . . . the dresses of five years ago, fashionable restaurants when the vogue has begun to ebb from them") were in the great promises—social, political, philosophical, technological, sensual—made by the past that the future, now one's own present, had not kept: the energies of one's sense of the betrayal of the past by the future and of the promises that remained to be kept.[3] The past was a funfair, a playground: you can feel Benjamin, Aragon, Ruttmann, and Chtcheglov skipping past their streets and shopwindows, and even Adorno hopping from one torture chamber to another. The modern was a cracking, a verge in time where historical time had lost its grip, a vortex of permanent crisis, jeopardy, and opportunity, the modern man or woman trapped in an elevator where with one hand he or she could touch the belief that all could be won and with the other the certainty that all could be lost. And hanging over all of this was the

3. Walter Benjamin, "Surrealism," in *One-Way Street and Other Writings*, trans. Edmund Jephcott (London: NLB, 1979), 229.

apprehension of the modern, which was about freedom, about one's own thoughts, one's own will, one's own actions, exercised alone or in concert, and the apprehension of its double, which was about the suppression of all of those attributes of the modern, or, with far more subtlety, the dismantling of the aura of reality adhering to them: what Adorno, in the first pages of *Minima Moralia*, described as the "claim to totality, which would suffer nothing to remain outside it."[4] If the technics of this antimodern were unlimited in their capacity for oppression, brutality, and evil, for erasing the very understanding of the modern of what it meant to be human, one thing that linked Benjamin, Aragon, Adorno, and Chtchelgov (and, for a moment, Ruttmann, before he became a Nazi) was the philosophical conviction, or instinct, that the totality had to be resisted, even chipped away, even defeated, by the fragment: the street, the sign, the name, the face, the aphorism, the evanescent, the ephemeral, the worthless, the unimportant, the meaningless. "What form do you suppose a life would take that was determined at a decisive moment by the street song last on everyone's lips?"[5]

That sentence, from Benjamin's 1929 essay "Surrealism," is the image, the dramatic moment, that he is searching for all through *One-Way Street*. A walk down the

4. Theodor Adorno, *Minima Moralia: Reflections from Damaged Life* (1951), trans. Edmund Jephcott (London: Verso, 2005), 16.

5. Benjamin, "Surrealism," 229.

street is also a quest: a quest to find, as Edmund Wilson wrote in 1922 in Paris, sharing time and space with the rest, "for what drama our setting is the setting." And he too caught the process, the way of thinking, that Benjamin would affirm in *One-Way Street*, shop by shop, building by building, hoarding by hoarding: "what bitter and terrific cost for a few commonplaces!" [6]

A few commonplaces—or, as Benjamin wrote in *One-Way Street*'s "Post No Bills," in the second-to-last entry in "The Critic's Technique in Thirteen Theses," "the art of the critic in a nutshell: to coin slogans without betraying ideas." [7] Those slogans were themselves fragments, bets against the future. In Europe, as the 1920s bent toward its end, anyone could see it, including those who looked away, who worked to convince themselves it wasn't true: the momentum was all toward what was not yet called totalitarianism, and the embrace of the fragment, its investigation, its interrogation, the affirmation of the fragment's truth and beauty, was an instinctive if not always political or aesthetic resistance. Mussolini, Stalin, Hitler, and Adorno's faceless capitalist totality made one argument about life: the whole explains the fragment. Benjamin countered: the fragment reveals the whole—and, like a tiny mammal scurrying under the feet of dinosaurs, escapes it. Looking back at the ruins, Adorno

6. Edmund Wilson, "Night Thoughts in Paris: A Rhapsody," *New Republic*, March 15, 1922, 77, 76.

7. *One-Way Street*, 50.

consciously walked in Benjamin's footsteps as he made his own book: "The whole is the false."[8]

Wish I didn't know now what I didn't know then: looking back on what his dead friend knew then, Adorno grasped for the ephemeral: "If the invention of the printing press inaugurated the bourgeois era, the time is at hand for its repeal by the mimeograph."[9] But Benjamin had more than been there first. Speaking in *One-Way Street* of what Mallarmé, "in his hermetic room, had discovered through a preestablished harmony with all the decisive events of our times in economics, technology, and public life"—the discovery that everything was falling to pieces—Benjamin means to turn up the volume.

> Script—having found, in the book, a refuge in which it can lead an autonomous existence—is pitilessly dragged out into the street by advertisements and subjected to the brutal heteronomies of economic chaos. This is the hard schooling of its new form. If centuries ago it began gradually to lie down, passing from the upright inscription to the manuscript resting on sloping desks before finally taking itself to bed in the printed book, it now begins just as slowly to rise again from the ground. The newspaper is read more in the vertical than in the horizontal plane, while film and advertisement

8. Adorno, *Minima Moralia*, 50.

9. Ibid., 51.

force the printed word entirely into the dictatorial perpendicular.[10]

That "rising from the ground"—he's describing a horror movie (in the 1910 Edison Studios *Frankenstein*, the monster rises from a cauldron). His words presage their own horror movie: "force," "dictatorial." If the momentum of the times was toward totalitarianism, *One-Way Street* gathers its own momentum. "Locust swarms of print, which already eclipse the sun of what city dwellers take for intellect" is less an argument than writing for its own sake, for its own pleasure.[11] In "Manorially Furnished Ten-Room Apartment," where Benjamin could be scripting Max Ernst's 1927 graphic murder mystery, *The Hundred Headless Woman*, he is speaking the same language, and the charge is the same:

> The furniture style of the second half of the nineteenth century has received its only adequate description, and analysis, in a certain type of detective novel at the dynamic center of which stands the horror of apartments. The arrangement of the furniture is at the same time the site plan of deadly traps, and the suites of rooms prescribes the path of the fleeing victim. That this kind of detective novel begins with Poe—at a time when such accommodations hardly yet existed—is no counterargument. For without exception the great writers

10. *One-Way Street*, 42–43.

11. Ibid.

perform their combinations in a world that comes after them, just as the Paris streets of Baudelaire's poems, as well as Dostoevsky's characters, existed only after 1900. The bourgeois interior of the 1860s to the 1890s—with its gigantic sideboards distended with carvings, the sunless corners where palms sit, the balcony embattled behind its balustrade, and the long corridors with their singing gas flames—fittingly houses only the corpse. . . . The soulless luxury of the furnishings becomes true comfort only in the presence of a dead body.[12]

Here you can feel that the argument is only an excuse for the pleasure of the hard-boiled writing, and the writing not in service of any argument but that of the pleasure of its own form. For despite the desperation and rage in "Imperial Panorama," subtitled "A Tour through the German Inflation"—which almost matches the dadaist Richard Huelsenbeck's 1920 *Deutstchland muss untergehen!* (Germany must fall!)—

Why the Germans followed Hitler

what completes the isolation of Germany in the eyes of other Europeans, what really engenders the attitude that, in dealing with the Germans, they are dealing with Hottentots (as it has been aptly put)—is the violence, incomprehensible to outsiders and wholly imperceptible to those imprisoned by it, with which circumstances, squalor, and

12. Ibid., 25–26.

> stupidity here subjugate people entirely to collective forces, as the lives of savages alone are subjected to tribal laws

—again it is the thrill of the writing, the way you can feel the writer caught up in the excitement of his own writing, reaching that spot where the way that words come together sparks the argument and the argument pushes the words to find their harmony, that pulls the reader into *One-Way Street*. And that the argument is complete as an argument— "The most European of all accomplishments," Benjamin continues in the next sentence,

> that more or less discernable irony with which the life of the individual asserts the right to run its course independently of the community into which it is cast, has completely deserted the Germans[13]

—can be almost lost in the heat of the prose.

It isn't lost. In this passage is the freedom the book seeks as it walks down its street, as it calls the street into being by walking it: in these words the book is in fact running its own course. An American would say "running its race"—but this is, as Benjamin insists, a European attribute, which demands a more fatalistic word.

> *This street is named*
> *Asja Lacis Street*

13. Ibid., 36.

after her who
as an engineer
cut it through the author

—so reads the opening epigraph of the book, and the erotic swath it cuts through any reader's expectations of any book signals where the book means to go. As a phantom in the book, Lacis—the Soviet dramatist who was for Benjamin the love of his life as he was a summer fling for her—opens every door on the street, the men's shop, the Mexican Embassy, the Lost-and-Found Office, the space for rent, the place closed for alterations, onto the whole of Europe, where she, like freedom, the chance to run one's own course, might be waiting. There are banalities all through the book— pressing back against the vertical plane of newspapers, Benjamin himself was writing short pieces for the papers in the mid-twenties, many of which found their way into *One-Way Street* (such portentous, meaningless pronouncements as "Work on good prose has three steps: a musical stage when it is composed, an architectonic one when it is built, and a textile one when it is woven," a whole section on how books and whores are alike, or "In summer, fat people are conspicuous; in winter, thin"[14]). They are as irritating as the people jostling you as you walk down the street, a dose of the quotidian, so that, again and again, each door opening onto a field of wonder (on the child, where "everything seemingly happens to him by chance") or terror ("the post-

14. Ibid., 69.

mark is the night side of stamps. . . . No sadistic fantasy can equal the black practice that covers faces with weals, and cleaves the land of entire continents like an earthquake"[15]), or disgust (not the relationship between but the equation of a mob and rising prices, where "No one sees further than the back before him, and each is proud to be thus exemplary for the eyes behind"[16]) makes it impossible for the reader to say he or she has no idea what the writer is talking about. The uncanny power of the book is that, regardless of one's time and place, a continuity from Benjamin's to one's own is plain. Just as Benjamin, Aragon, Ruttmann, Adorno, Chtcheglov, and so many others were, within their thirty-year temporal circle, speaking the same language, one cannot read through the noisiest pages in *One-Way Street* without recognizing oneself.

That has to do, in part, with the way time works in *One-Way Street*. "Between 1865 and 1875," Benjamin wrote in 1929, the year after *One-Way Street* appeared, "a number of great anarchists, without knowing of each other, worked on their infernal machines. And the astonishing thing is that independently of one another they set its clock at exactly the same hour, and forty years later in Western Europe the writings of Dostoevsky, Rimbaud, and Lautréamont exploded at the same time."[17] In other words, time slips in *One-Way Street*, just as it does in Laura Oldfield Ford's *Savage Messiah*,

15. Ibid., 58, 80.

16. Ibid., 45.

17. Benjamin, "Surrealism," 234.

Ford making her way down an unnamed street, one of those streets, as De Quincey wrote of his own wanderings, where one could doubt "whether they had yet been laid down in the modern charts of London,"[18] and the city reveals itself: "As I lay my palm flat against the wall I grasp past texts never fully erasing the traces of earlier inscriptions."[19] It is the little critical bomb Benjamin planted in *One-Way Street*, where Baudelaire's streets and Dostoevsky's characters don't appear until decades after Baudelaire and Dostoevsky are dead: "without exception the great writers perform their combinations in a world that comes after them."

That doesn't mean, I don't think, that, as Bob Dylan has said of the 1930s Mississippi blues singer Robert Johnson, Benjamin was writing "for an audience that only he could see, one off in the future."[20] It means that the fragment exerts its own gravity, that each fragment contains its own time, and that great writers thus inhabit the past, the present, and the future at once, without a sense of time passing, everything swirling around them, speaking in a babble that

18. Thomas De Quincey, *Confessions of an English Opium-Eater* (1821) (New York: Penguin Books, 1981), 81.

19. Laura Oldfield Ford, *Savage Messiah* (London: Verso, 2011), unpaginated, quoted in Greil Marcus, "Real Life Rock Top Ten," *Believer*, July–August 2012.

20. Bob Dylan, *Chronicles*, vol. 1 (New York: Simon and Schuster, 2004), 285.

the writer might, if he or she can, for a moment turn back into the single tongue humanity spoke before God scattered it. In *One-Way Street* the mind is constantly at play, thinking, dreaming, thinking about dreaming, free-associating, not distinguishing between the trivial and the world-historical, the modern mind trying to walk and psychoanalyze itself and the world at the same time. No wonder the book has so many traveling companions: Benjamin is tapping into an essential modernist impulse, to remake the world out of attractive, invaluable fragments, bits of what Aragon called "the cult of the ephemeral," those things that to nonmodernists appear to be merely part of the unassailable whole.[21]

One-Way Street is a performance; it is an experiment; it is a work permanently in progress. It is the distillation of the credo Benjamin set down in 1934: "An author who teaches a writer nothing teaches nobody anything. The determining factor is the exemplary character of a production that enables it, first, to lead other producers to this production, and secondly to present them with an improved apparatus for their use. And this apparatus is better to the degree that it leads consumers to production, in short that it is capable of making co-workers out of readers or spectators."[22] It is an invitation to the apprehension of one's own modernity.

21. Aragon, *Paris Peasant*, 14.

22. Walter Benjamin, "The Author as Producer" (1934), trans. John Heckman, *New Left Review*, July–August 1970.

ONE-WAY STREET

INTRODUCTION

Michael W. Jennings

When it appeared in 1928, Walter Benjamin's *One-Way Street* presented the reader with a new and radical literary form.[1] Avoiding all semblance of linear narrative, the book seems on first reading to offer a jumble of sixty apparently autonomous short prose pieces: aphorisms, jokes, dream protocols; cityscapes, landscapes, and mindscapes; portions of writing manuals; trenchant contemporary political analysis; prescient appreciations of the child's psychology, behavior, and moods; decodings of bourgeois fashion, living arrangements, and courtship patterns; and, time and again, remarkable penetrations into the heart of everyday things, what Benjamin would later call the empathy with "the soul of the commodity."[2] The book's title indicates the organizing conceit of this apparent textual miscellany: the names of the individual sections evoke the dense urban environment along a street, with its apartments, shops, services, construction sites, embassies, monuments, and pleasure palaces. Benjamin's street is alive with fluttering flags, clocks, and especially public inscriptions: signs, advertisements

1. The early stages of the conceptualization of this essay were the product of a collaboration with Miriam Bratu Hansen, to whom this volume is dedicated.

2. Walter Benjamin, *The Arcades Project*, trans. Howard Eiland and Kevin McLaughlin (Cambridge, MA: Harvard University Press, 1999), 369.

and posters, mottos, sayings, and slogans. And the textual diversity of *One-Way Street* ensures that the street resonates with the hubbub of many voices, with what Lionel Trilling once called the great "hum and buzz" of social interaction. Benjamin's built environment, his "one-way street," is a thoroughfare that requires not just mental agility but especially a kind of modern urban literacy.

Many of the pieces in *One-Way Street* first appeared in the feuilleton section—not a separate section, but rather an area at the bottom of every page—of newspapers and magazines, and the spatial restrictions of the feuilleton played a decisive role in the shaping of the prose form on which the book is based.[3] In the course of the 1920s, a number of prominent writers—many of them Benjamin's friends, like Ernst Bloch and Siegfried Kracauer—shaped their writing practice in order to accommodate it to the feuilleton; the *kleine Form* or "little form" that resulted came rapidly to be identified as the primary mode of cultural commentary and criticism in the Weimar Republic.[4] Benjamin's adaptation of the form stood apart in crucial ways, though, from that of many of his contemporaries. A number of the short prose pieces in *One-Way Street* are shaped by Benjamin's fascination with the aphorism as form. Some of his favorite writers—Georg Chris-

3. On the feuilleton and its role in the shaping of Benjamin's prose, see Howard Eiland and Michael W. Jennings, *Walter Benjamin: A Critical Life* (Cambridge, MA: Harvard University Press, 2014), 258.

4. On the "little form" see ibid., 259, and especially Eckard Köhn, *Strassenrausch: Flanerie und kleine Form: Versuch zur Literaturgeschichte des Flaneurs bis 1933* (Berlin: Das Arsenal, 1989).

toph Lichtenberg, the German Romantic writers Friedrich Schlegel and Novalis, and above all Friedrich Nietzsche—had added a new philosophical bite to the aphorism's characteristic presentation as condensed moral or psychological insight. Those sections of *One-Way Street* that come closest to the aphorism are in fact Benjamin's earliest experiments with the *Denkbild* or figure of thought, the philosophically charged miniature that would in the 1930s become his characteristic mode of expression.[5] Just as important, though, for the shape of the text was Benjamin's initial foray into the European avant-garde movements of the mid-1920s. His participation in 1923 and 1924 in the avant-garde cenacle known today as the "G Group" led him to search for a prose form that could approximate the trenchancy of the surrealist gloss and for a larger prose structure that could approximate the complexity of the Dadaist photomontage.[6]

The first section of *One-Way Street*, "Filling Station," already issues a call to arms for the little form in its avant-garde manifestation: "Significant literary effectiveness . . . must nurture the inconspicuous forms that fit its influence

5. On the *Denkbild*, see especially Gerhard Richter, *Thought-Images: Frankfurt School Writers' Reflections from Damaged Life* (Stanford, CA: Stanford University Press, 2007).

6. On Benjamin's participation in the avant-garde, see Michael Jennings, "Walter Benjamin and the European Avant-Garde," in *The Cambridge Companion to Walter Benjamin*, ed. David S. Ferris (Cambridge, UK: Cambridge University Press, 2004), 18–34. On the G Group, see Michael Jennings and Detlef Mertins, *G: An Avant-Garde Journal of Art, Architecture, Design, and Film, 1923–1926* (Los Angeles: Getty Research Institute, 2010).

in active communities better than does the pretentious, universal gesture of the book—in leaflets, brochures, articles, and placards. Only this prompt language shows itself actively equal to the moment" (21). In a series of rapid claims in the sections to come, Benjamin privileges the fragment over the finished work ("the work is the death mask of its conception" [47]), improvisation over "competence" ("all the decisive blows are struck left-handed" [27]), and waste products and detritus over the carefully crafted (children bring together "materials of widely different kinds in a new, intuitive relationship") (31). Traditional forms of writing were, for Benjamin, simply no longer capable of surviving in capitalist modernity—let alone of providing the framework for meaningful insights into its structure, functioning, and effects. Thus the juxtaposition of seemingly antithetical forms: surrealist-inspired dream protocols stand next to examples of a writerly constructivism, as when Benjamin claims that writing "will suddenly take possession of an adequate material content" in "statistical and technical diagrams" (43).

For all the beauty, piercing insight, and originality of the individual pieces in *One-Way Street*, though, the book places inordinate demands upon the reader. The lack of any apparent organizing logic, together with the remarkable thematic and formal diversity of the collection, means that most readers simply proceed seriatim, encountering the sections in the order in which they are printed. Yet Benjamin's text is highly structured. Far from a loose aggregation of prose aperçus, *One-Way Street* represents Benjamin's first attempt to create a text as a highly theorized constellation of fragments. In order to understand his strategy, it is important to realize that *One-Way Street* was written *together* with his epochal study of the Baroque "play of mourning," *Origin of German Trauerspiel.* There, in the notoriously refractory "Epistemo-Critical Preface," Benjamin presents a theory of writing—a theory that, if anything, has more pertinence for a reading of *One-Way Street* than for one of the *Trauerspiel* book. In characterizing his own text as a "tractatus" or treatise, he contrasts its paratactic form and logic with that of the essay, with its linear, hypotactic construction of an argument:

> Method is indirection. Presentation as indirection, the roundabout way—this, then, is the methodological character of the tractatus. Renunciation of the unbroken course of intention is its immediately distinguishing feature. With its staying power, thinking constantly begins anew; with its sense of the circumstantial, it goes back to the thing itself. This unceasing inhale-and-exhale is the form of existence most proper to contemplation. . . . Just as the majesty of mosaics remains when they are capriciously disassembled, so philosophical observation fears no dissipation of momentum. Out of the singular and disparate they come together; nothing could attest more powerfully to the transcendent impact— whether of the saint's image or of the truth.[7]

7. Walter Benjamin, *Origin of German Trauerspiel,* ed. and trans. Howard Eiland and Michael W. Jennings (Cambridge, MA: Harvard University Press, 2016).

Benjamin's construction of this "roundabout way" in *One-Way Street* is indebted to the principles of photomontage developed by the Berlin Dadaists. The *Klebebilder*, literally "pasted pictures," of the Dadaists consisted of images and parts of images cut directly out of popular print media, and especially the "illustrated newspapers"; these image shards bearing traces of everyday life were then pasted, sometimes together with other materials, onto a background. The photomontage demanded a new kind of image reading: without the structures provided by single-point perspective and perspectival recession into space, the viewer is forced to form a mental image of the picture, an image that is often a free recombination of spatially dispersed elements of the photomontage. Benjamin comments on the possibility of a work composed of "mutilated" portions of larger wholes in "Stamp Shop".[8] "Stamps bristle with tiny numbers, minute letters, diminutive leaves and eyes. They are graphic cellular tissue. All this swarms about and, like lower animals, lives on even when mutilated. This is why such powerful pictures can be made of pieces of stamps stuck together [*zusammengeklebt*]" (80–81).

If the photomontage confronted the viewer with the imperative to see differently, Benjamin's use of the montage principle in a literary text demands that the reader *read differently.* The early reviews—several of them by Benjamin's

8. On the violence inherent in the photomontage practices of the Berlin Dadaists, see Brigid Doherty, "See: 'We Are All Neurasthenics!' or, the Trauma of Dada Montage," *Critical Inquiry* 24, no. 1 (Autumn 1997): 82–132.

friends and comrades in arms—in fact focused precisely on the new practices of reading demanded by the new, "indirect" structure of Benjamin's book. Franz Hessel: "The reader has to be alert, has to dodge, feels that thinking is a danger and that standing still in one's thoughts constitutes an obstacle to traffic." Ernst Bloch: "One goes along quite cheerfully. Then something disturbs us. Then something moves us against our will. It gleams, sharp and strange, seems to be something great, then, just to the side, becomes something wholly different."[9] The "roundabout way" of Benjamin's text, with its stops, starts, dodges, and resistances, suggests new pathways through the textual city at every turn, forces the reader to bring together passages that lie far apart in the text. This action, reading as constellating, is indebted to Benjamin's understanding of surrealism: the reader who "follows the movement of his mind in the free flight of daydreaming" is granted this freedom by the unusual malleability of Benjamin's text. Yet reading of this sort also demands a critical awareness, a new sort of mindedness, as the subliminal connections between textual passages are complimented by overt thematic and formal echoes and rhymes. In short, the reader is forced to think of the text as a constellation of disparate parts. Much later, Benjamin would attribute to the reading of texts as constellations the

9. Franz Hessel, "Walter Benjamin: Einbahnstraße," *Das Tagebuch* 9 (March 3, 1928), quoted in Walter Benjamin, *Einbahnstraße: Werke und Nachlaß*, vol. 8, ed. Detlev Schöttker (Frankfurt: Suhrkamp Verlag, 2009), 510. Ernst Bloch, "Revueform in der Philosophie," *Vossische Zeitung*, 182 (August 1, 1928), quoted in Benjamin, *Einbahnstraße*, 525.

imprint of the perilous critical moment on which all reading is founded.[10]

Yet Benjamin was aware that the "aerial perspective" of the constellation could afford only one view of the text. "Only he who walks the road on foot," he writes in the section "Chinese Curios," "learns of the power it commands" (27). And the reader walking down the textual street on foot of course must submit to the law of unidirectionality enforced by the one-way street. Standing at the top of this street, the linear reader looks down into what Benjamin in a letter called "a prospect of precipitous depth."[11] This readerly vertigo evokes, then, a particular experience of history. Movement down this one-way street is forced, inevitable: there is not only no turning back, there seems to be no turning aside. The reading experience, on this level, replicates the predominant experience of life under capitalist modernity, the sense of "impending catastrophe" in all of its inevitability that Benjamin describes in the central sociopolitical analysis of *One-Way Street*, the section "Imperial Panorama: A Tour through the German Inflation":

> The helpless fixation on notions of security and property deriving from past decades keeps the average citizen from perceiving the quite remarkable stabilities of an entirely new kind that underlie the

10. Benjamin, *The Arcades Project*, 462–463.

11. Walter Benjamin, *The Correspondence of Walter Benjamin*, trans. M. R. Jacobson and E. M. Jacobson (Chicago: University of Chicago Press, 1994), 306.

present situation. . . . But stable conditions need by
no means be pleasant conditions, and even before
the war there were strata for whom stabilized conditions were stabilized wretchedness. To decline is no
less stable, no more surprising, than to rise. Only a
view that acknowledges downfall as the sole reason
for the present situation can advance beyond enervating amazement at what is daily repeated, and
perceive the phenomena of decline as stability itself
and rescue alone as extraordinary, verging on the
marvelous and incomprehensible. (33)

The "power" of the textual road thus indeed "commands the
soul" of the linear reader; but, in one of the many reversals
that characterize the reading experience of *One-Way Street*,
that power proves to be destructive.

In this variegated search for new formal means to
evoke the experience of the modern urban street, Benjamin's text participates in a widespread and highly influen-
tial project of German experimental writing that began before the First World War and reached its culmination in the
Weimar Republic. The decade between 1910 and 1920 had
produced a remarkable series of prose experiments: Robert
Musil's stories "The Perfection of Love" and "The Tempta-
tion of Quiet Veronika" (1911), the art historian Carl Ein-
stein's novel *Bebuquin or the Dilettantes of the Miracle*
(1912), and Gottfried Benn's cycle of stories *Brains* (1916).
But in its conjuring of the modern metropolis, Benjamin's
book demands comparison above all with what is often re-

garded as the key novel of the Weimar Republic, Alfred Döblin's *Berlin Alexanderplatz* (1929). Benjamin and Döblin
insist, in similar ways, that the demands of contemporary
conditions be respected through an investigation of the
potentials of language as the medium for the immediate,
sensuous presentation of everyday things. Just as Benjamin
evokes these things through the titles of each section of his
text, Döblin inserts things—usually through descriptive language, but occasionally graphically—into his text without
commentary. He describes the task of the storyteller who de-
velops a "cinema style" as "not to narrate, but to build." It is
here that the similarity of approach between Döblin and
Benjamin ends: for Döblin, the mere representation of the
city and its aural and tactile energies is enough, while for
Benjamin the commodity—the primary element of the
modern urban capitalist environment—must be *theorized.*

One-Way Street shows a growing awareness on Benjamin's part of the disorienting and denaturing effects im-
posed on human consciousness by commodity fetishism. It
is in fact in *One-Way Street* that Benjamin initiates his sus-
tained attempt to theorize the commodity, building on the
theories of Karl Marx and Georg Lukacs; the full force
of that theory and its critique of capitalism will emerge only
in the essays of the 1930s associated with Benjamin's "Arcades Project."[12] On his reading of the desperate plight of

12. The most suggestive analysis of Benjamin's theory of commodities remains that of Terry Eagleton in *Walter Benjamin, or Towards a Revolutionary Criticism* (London: New Left Books, 1981).

the contemporary German, human faculties have fallen prey not merely to the confusions attendant on the hyperinflation that crippled the Weimar Republic, but also more generally to the influence of commodities, to the "boundless resistance of the outside world" (38):

> Warmth is ebbing from things. Objects of daily use gently but insistently repel us. Day by day, in overcoming the sum of secret resistances—not only the overt ones—that they put in our way, we have an immense labor to perform. We must compensate for their coldness with our warmth if they are not to freeze us to death, and handle their spiny forms with infinite dexterity if we are not to bleed to death. (38)

Benjamin's analysis of this power, what he later called the "sex-appeal of the anorganic,"[13] relies on his particular inflection of the concept of reification that he derives from Marx and Lukacs. Marx, in *Capital*, had attributed to the commodity—an apparently "very trivial thing, and easily understood"—"perceptible and imperceptible [*sinnlich übersinnlich*]" properties. Commodities appear to be "independent beings endowed with life, and entering into relation both with one another and the human race."[14] Marx attempted to explain this phenomenon metaphorically; he

13. Benjamin, *The Arcades Project*, 8.

14. Karl Marx, *Capital*, in Robert Tucker, ed., *The Marx-Engels Reader*, 2nd ed. (New York: W. W. Norton, 1978), 319–321.

referred to the propensity of commodities to form networks of significance and influence as their "fetishism," and implied that the fetishistic relationship that obtains between commodities and human consciousness cannot help but denature and distort our standpoint in the world. Benjamin signals his use of this concept early in *One-Way Street* in the section "Mexican Embassy." He there first quotes Baudelaire on the power of fetishes and then relates an anecdote of a missionary station in Mexico: "Toward a wooden bust of God the Father, fixed high on a wall of the cave, a priest raised a Mexican fetish. At this, the divine head turned thrice in denial from right to left" (29). He is also quite specific as to the direct effect of this fetishism on human perception and intellect. The primary characteristic of commodity fetishism is ambiguity: "All things, in an irreversible process of mingling and contamination, are losing their intrinsic character while ambiguity displaces authenticity" (39). Ambiguity is for Benjamin at once an epistemological and a moral category. The cognitive disorientation that results from encounters with the deeply ambiguous world of things prevents the human subject from an adequate moral agency and above all denies her an understanding of the world, the kind of understanding that can alone provide the capacity for resistance and social change.

In *One-Way Street*, the effects of this disorientation are rendered brilliantly: as space. In "Manorially Furnished Ten-Room Apartment," Benjamin asserts only partially scurrilously that the detective novel—of which he was an avid reader—arose out of the necessity of making clear the layout of the bourgeois apartment—a space rendered wholly irrational by the networks of commodities with which it is "furnished."[15] The apartment of the nineteenth century is replete with "gigantic sideboards distended with carvings, the sunless corners where potted palms sit," in short, "that rank Orient inhabiting their interiors: the Persian carpet and the ottoman, the hanging lamp and the genuine dagger from the Caucasus" (26). This space is marked by an insurmountable ambiguity. On the one hand hermetically sealed and unimaginably insular—the balcony is "embattled behind its balustrade"—the apartment is a fortress and a coffin. On the other hand, it is always also elsewhere, inhabiting a metaphorical Orient whose exoticism blurs and conceals the mundanity of the real surroundings. The inhabitant is at once trapped and eternally escaping, subject to a spatial disorientation that robs his existence of solidity and authenticity. This succumbing to irrationality can prove fatal: "Behind the heavy, gathered Khilim tapestries, the master of the house has orgies with his share certificates, feels himself the eastern merchant, the indolent pasha in the caravanserai of otiose enchantment, until that dagger in its silver sling above the divan puts an end, one fine afternoon, to his siesta and himself" (26). Perhaps the most brilliant evocation of this form of spatial displacement occurs toward the end of the volume, in "Stand-Up Beer

15. Tom Gunning, "The Exterior as Intérieur: Benjamin's Optical Detective," *boundary* 2 30, no. 1 (Spring 2003): 105–129.

Hall." There, sailors are suggested as the most telling examples of the influence of commodities, as they and their
power are organized and deployed by international capital.
"Imbued to the marrow with the international norms of
industry, they are not the dupes of palms and icebergs" (92).
The bourgeoisie experience the disorienting power in a mediated manner; their forced exoticism is only an indirect
result. For the sailor, however, whose work "maintains contact with the commodities in the hull of the ship," the
world actually traveled and lived in ceases to have any
local character. "The city sights are not seen but bought.
In the sailors' chests, the leather belt from Hong Kong is
juxtaposed with a panorama of Palermo and a girl's photo
from Stettin. . . . He lives on the open sea in a city where,
on the Marseilles Cannebière, a Port Said bar stands diagonally opposite a Hamburg brothel" (92). "And listening to
them, one realizes what mendacity resides in voyaging" (93).

Here, and throughout his career, though, Benjamin
will insist on a fundamentally *double* potential inherent in
our encounters with the things that constitute our everyday
modernity. Things not only exert a baleful influence upon
human consciousness and perception: they also hold within
themselves a critical, potentially revolutionary potential as
well. The new attestation of the critical potentials of things
emerged in the mid-1920s as Benjamin, in close collaboration with his friend Siegfried Kracauer, embarked on a
project that sought to invent the criticism of popular culture
as a form, and in fact as a privileged form of social analy-

sis.[16] *One-Way Street* contains a number of Benjamin's earliest attempts to derive from a reading of a seemingly debased object a new perceptual or political potential. In "These Spaces for Rent," he chronicles the obsolescence of criticism, with its basis in a ratiocination and contemplation that have been deeply tainted under capitalism, and its replacement through . . . advertising:

> Today the most real, mercantile gaze into the heart of things is the advertisement. It tears down the stage upon which contemplation moved, and all but hits us between the eyes with things as a car, growing to gigantic proportions, careens at us out of a film screen. And just as the film does not present furniture and façades in completed forms for critical inspection, . . . the genuine advertisement hurls things at us with the tempo of a good film. . . . For the man in the street, however, it is money that affects him in this way, brings him into perceived contact with things. . . . The warmth of the subject is communicated to him, stirs sentient springs. What, in the end, makes advertisements so superior to criticism? Not what the moving red neon sign says—but the fiery pool reflecting it in the asphalt. (76–77)

16. Michael Jennings, "Walter Benjamin, Siegfried Kracauer, and Weimar Criticism," in *Weimar Thought: A Contested Legacy*, ed. Peter Gordon and John McCormack (Princeton, NJ: Princeton University Press, 2013), 203–219.

Walter Benjamin was attuned, in other words, to a doubleness that he found in all things, to their devastating effect
on human consciousness *and* to their critical potential. As
he would put it in his essay on surrealism (1929), there are
"revolutionary energies" slumbering in the "world of things."[17]
These energies hardly reveal themselves, however, to a
human perception shaped by life under capitalism. An
important thematic arc in *One-Way Street* delineates a
number of alternative modes of perception. Perhaps unsur-
prisingly, children's perception, as yet untainted by the world
of adults, is accorded a privileged place. In "Construction
Site," children, alert to the hidden potentials of "waste products," "bring together, in the artifact produced in play, materials of widely differing kinds in a new, intuitive relationship" (31). And in "Enlargements," the world reveals itself in
new ways—"space begins to stammer and the trees to
come to their senses"—to the child riding on a carousel
(57). As the remarks above have suggested, new forms of
writing—and reading—also bear within them new perceptual potentials. "Writing," Benjamin claims in "Attested
Auditor of Books," "advancing ever more deeply into the
graphic regions of its new eccentric figurativeness, will suddenly take possession of an adequate material content" (43).
And finally, Benjamin inaugurates in *One-Way Street* a
problematic that will come to dominate his thought in the

17. Walter Benjamin, "Surrealism," in *Selected Writings*, vol. 2, ed. Michael W. Jennings, Howard Eiland, and Gary Smith (Cambridge, MA:
Harvard University Press, 1999), 207–221.

1930s: the hidden potentials of new technologies and technological media, even those that seem only to participate in the ongoing disorientation of human consciousness: "The typewriter will alienate the hand of the man of letters from the pen only when the precision of typographic forms has directly entered the conception of his books. One might suppose that new systems with more variable typefaces would then be needed. They will replace the pliancy of the hand with the innervation of commanding fingers" (45). The concept of innervation—the production in humans of a new neurophysiological receptivity to heretofore hidden aspects of the world—appears here for the first time in Benjamin's work, and will emerge as the heuristic horizon toward which much of his thinking on media and experience will tend in the 1930s.[18]

In *One-Way Street*, the repeated discovery of this fundamental doubleness prepares for the emergence of a final thematic arc that comes to dominate the book's final pages: the theme of an eroticized, somatic reception that might provide the basis for a new form of collectivity—or might lead to cataclysm. In an important way, this theme provides the bridge between the all-important social analysis of "Imperial Panorama" at the book's center and the book's grand, symphonic conclusion in "To the Planetarium." In "Imperial Panorama," humans are presented

18. On the concept of innervation, see especially Miriam Bratu Hansen, *Cinema and Experience: Siegfried Kracauer, Walter Benjamin, and Theodor W. Adorno* (Berkeley: University of California Press, 2012), 132–162.

as denatured and imperiled, but without any sense for the true nature of the danger that imperils them. The awakening of that sense of danger—the prerequisite to any meaningful change—lies, as he puts it in "Madame Ariane: Second Courtyard on the Left," in the acquisition of "presence of mind" and "precise awareness of the present moment." And if these are to be achieved, if "the threatening future" is to be turned into a "fulfilled 'now,'" that presence of mind must be *bodily*: "Scipio, stumbling as he set foot on Carthaginian soil, cried out, spreading his arms wide as he fell, the watchword of victory, 'Teneo te, terra Africana!' What would have become a portent of disaster he binds bodily to the moment, making himself the factotum of his body" (88–89). It must be said that Benjamin's sense of bodilyness all too often entails the juxtaposition of progressive ideas with a language of eroticism that ranges from the merely heterosexist to the frankly misogynistic. The text speaks, in other words, with the masculinist voice of the avant-garde. And that voice is nowhere more suggestive—and nowhere more problematic—than in "To the Planetarium," the piece that closes *One-Way Street*.

"To the Planetarium" is symphonic in its attempt to tie together the main discursive strands of the book as a whole: the role of technology in the "relation between nature and man"; the eroticism that makes possible the "ecstatic trance" and a "new and unprecedented commingling with the cosmic powers"; and, finally, the doubled potentials of our contact with things:

> In the nights of annihilation of the last war, the
> frame of mankind was shaken by a feeling that re-
> sembled the bliss of the epileptic. And the revolts
> that followed it were the first attempt of mankind
> to bring the new body under its control. The power
> of the proletariat is the measure of its convales-
> cence. If it is not gripped to the very marrow by
> the discipline of this power, no pacifist polemics
> will save it. Living substance conquers the frenzy
> of destruction only in the ecstasy of procreation.
> (95–96)

More than any other text by Benjamin, "To the Planetarium"
reveals the dissonances and contradictions that arose from
the confrontation of his early work with his later thought on
experience, media, and politics. The discourse of an ecstatic
commingling with the cosmos betrays his ongoing fascination with vitalist philosophy and in particular with the
thought of Ludwig Klages.[19] If we take every aspect of the
text seriously, then we must acknowledge that Benjamin
comes to the scandalous conclusion that the revolutions at
the end of the war—the October Revolution in Russia and

19. Benjamin had known Klages since his days in the Youth Movement
before World War I. Klages's text *Vom kosmogonischen Eros* had appeared
in 1921. Until late into the 1930s Benjamin hoped to be able to write an
analysis of the concept of the archetype in Klages and C. G. Jung. On
Benjamin's relationship to Klages and to vitalism more generally, see
Nitzan Lebovic, "The Terror and Beauty of Lebensphilosophie: Ludwig
Klages, Walter Benjamin, and Alfred Bauemler," *South Central Review*
23, no. 1 (Spring 2006): 23–39.

the November Revolution in Germany—had as their pre-
condition a new body politic forged in the "bliss" that
emerged as the war shook mankind to its roots.[20] As Greil
Marcus notes in the Preface, *One-Way Street* is not without
its blind spots—or, to stay with the urban metaphor, its dead
ends. Yet the attentive reader can be gripped, if not in ecstasy, then certainly "to the marrow" by Benjamin's first attempt at a montage book.

20. Benjamin's is hardly an isolated claim. Robert Musil makes a similar
claim in the 1921 essay "Nation, as Ideal and as Reality," in Musil, *Precision and Soul: Essays and Addresses*, ed. and trans. Burton Pike and Robert
S. Luft (Chicago: University of Chicago Press, 1995), 101–115.

ONE-WAY STREET

This street is named
Asja Lacis Street
after her who
as an engineer
cut it through the author

Filling Station

The construction of life is at present in the power far more of facts than of convictions, and of such facts as have scarcely ever become the basis of convictions. Under these circumstances, true literary activity cannot aspire to take place within a literary framework; this is, rather, the habitual expression of its sterility. Significant literary effectiveness can come into being only in a strict alternation between action and writing; it must nurture the inconspicuous forms that fit its influence in active communities better than does the pretentious, universal gesture of the book—in leaflets, brochures, articles, and placards. Only this prompt language shows itself actively equal to the moment. Opinions are to the vast apparatus of social existence what oil is to machines: one does not go up to a turbine and pour machine oil over it; one applies a little to hidden spindles and joints that one has to know.

Breakfast Room

A popular tradition warns against recounting dreams the next morning on an empty stomach. In this state, though awake, one remains under the spell of the dream. For washing brings only the surface of the body and the visible motor functions into the light, while in the deeper strata, even during the morning ablutions, the gray penumbra of dream persists and, indeed, in the solitude of the first waking hour, consolidates itself. He who shuns contact with the day, whether for fear of his fellow men or for the sake of inward composure, is unwilling to eat and disdains his breakfast. He thus avoids a rupture between the nocturnal and the daytime worlds—a precaution justified only by the combustion of dream in a concentrated morning's work, if not in prayer; otherwise this avoidance can be a source of confusion between vital rhythms. In this condition, the narration of dreams can bring calamity, because a person still half in league with the dream world betrays it in his words and must incur its revenge. To express this in more modern terms: he betrays himself. He has outgrown the protection of dreaming naïveté, and in laying hands on his dream visages without thinking, he surrenders himself. For only from the far bank, from broad daylight, may dream be addressed from the superior vantage of memory. This further side of dream is attainable only through a cleansing analogous to washing, yet totally different. By way of the stomach. The fasting man tells his dream as if he were talking in his sleep.

Number 113[1]

The hours that hold the figure and the form
Have run their course within the house of dream.

CELLAR

We have long forgotten the ritual by which the house of our
life was erected. But when it is under assault and enemy
bombs are already taking their toll, what enervated, perverse
antiquities do they not lay bare in the foundations! What
things were interred and sacrificed amid magic incantations,
what horrible cabinet of curiosities lies there below, where
the deepest shafts are reserved for what is most common-
place? In a night of despair, I dreamed I was with my best
friend from my schooldays (whom I had not seen for decades and had scarcely ever thought of at that time), tempes-
tuously renewing our friendship and brotherhood. But
when I awoke, it became clear that what despair had brought
to light like a detonation was the corpse of that boy, who had
been immured as a warning: that whoever one day lives here
may in no respect resemble him.

VESTIBULE

A visit to Goethe's house.[2] I cannot recall having seen
rooms in the dream. It was a perspective of whitewashed
corridors like those in a school. Two elderly English lady
visitors and a curator are the dream's extras. The curator
requests us to sign the visitors' book lying open on a desk

at the farthest end of a passage. On reaching it, I find as I turn the pages my name already entered in big, unruly, childish characters.

DINING HALL

In a dream I saw myself in Goethe's study. It bore no resemblance to the one in Weimar. Above all, it was very small and had only one window. The side of the writing desk abutted on the wall opposite the window. Sitting and writing at it was the poet, in extreme old age. I was standing to one side when he broke off to give me a small vase, an urn from antiquity, as a present. I turned it between my hands. An immense heat filled the room. Goethe rose to his feet and accompanied me to an adjoining chamber, where a table was set for my relatives. It seemed prepared, however, for many more than their number. Doubtless there were places for my ancestors, too. At the end, on the right, I sat down beside Goethe. When the meal was over, he rose with difficulty, and by gesturing I sought leave to support him. Touching his elbow, I began to weep with emotion.

For Men

To convince is to conquer without conception.

Standard Clock

To great writers, finished works weigh lighter than those fragments on which they work throughout their lives. For only the more feeble and distracted take an inimitable pleasure in closure, feeling that their lives have thereby been given back to them. For the genius each caesura, and the heavy blows of fate, fall like gentle sleep itself into his workshop labor. Around it he draws a charmed circle of fragments. "Genius is application."

Come Back! All Is Forgiven!

Like someone performing the giant swing on the horizontal bar, each boy spins for himself the wheel of fortune from which, sooner or later, the momentous lot shall fall. For only that which we knew or practiced at fifteen will one day constitute our attraction. And one thing, therefore, can never be made good: having neglected to run away from one's parents. From forty-eight hours' exposure in those years, as if in a caustic solution, the crystal of life's happiness forms.

Manorially Furnished Ten-Room Apartment

The furniture style of the second half of the nineteenth century has received its only adequate description, and analysis, in a certain type of detective novel at the dynamic center of which stands the horror of apartments. The arrangement of the furniture is at the same time the site plan of deadly traps, and the suite of rooms prescribes the path of the fleeing victim. That this kind of detective novel begins with Poe—at a time when such accommodations hardly yet existed—is no counterargument. For without exception the great writers perform their combinations in a world that comes after them, just as the Paris streets of Baudelaire's poems, as well as Dostoevsky's characters, existed only after 1900. The bourgeois interior of the 1860s to the 1890s— with its gigantic sideboards distended with carvings, the sunless corners where potted palms sit, the balcony embattled behind its balustrade, and the long corridors with their singing gas flames—fittingly houses only the corpse. "On this sofa the aunt cannot but be murdered." The soulless luxury of the furnishings becomes true comfort only in the presence of a dead body. Far more interesting than the Oriental landscapes in detective novels is that rank Orient inhabiting their interiors: the Persian carpet and the ottoman, the hanging lamp and the genuine dagger from the Caucasus. Behind the heavy, gathered Khilim tapestries, the master of the house has orgies with his share certificates, feels himself the eastern merchant, the indolent pasha in the caravanserai of otiose enchantment, until that dagger in its silver sling above the divan puts an end, one fine afternoon, to his siesta and himself. This character of the bourgeois apartment, tremulously awaiting the nameless murderer like a lascivious old lady her gallant, has been penetrated by a number of authors who, as writers of "detective stories"—and perhaps also because in their works part of the bourgeois pandemonium is exhibited—have been denied the reputation they deserve. The quality in question has been captured in isolated writings by Conan Doyle and in a major work by A. K. Green.[3] And with *The*

Phantom of the Opera, one of the great novels about the nineteenth century, Gaston Leroux has brought the genre to its apotheosis.[4]

Chinese Curios

These are days when no one should rely unduly on his "competence." Strength lies in improvisation. All the decisive blows are struck left-handed.

At the beginning of the long downhill lane that leads to the house of ——, whom I visited each evening, is a gate. After she moved, the opening of its archway henceforth stood before me like an ear that has lost the power of hearing.

A child in his nightshirt cannot be prevailed upon to greet an arriving visitor. Those present, invoking a higher moral standpoint, admonish him in vain to overcome his prudery. A few minutes later he reappears, now stark naked, before the visitor. In the meantime he has washed.

The power of a country road when one is walking along it is different from the power it has when one is flying over it by airplane. In the same way, the power of a text when it is read is different from the power it has when it is copied out. The airplane passenger sees only how the road pushes through the landscape, how it unfolds according to the same laws as the terrain surrounding it. Only he who walks the road on foot learns of the power it commands, and of how, from the very scenery that for the flier is only the unfurled plain, it calls forth distances, belvederes, clearings, prospects at each of its turns like a commander deploying soldiers at a front. Only the copied text thus commands the soul of him who is occupied with it, whereas the mere reader never discovers the new aspects of his inner self that are opened by the text, that road cut through the interior jungle forever closing behind it: because the reader follows the movement of his mind in the free flight of daydreaming, whereas the copier submits it to command. The Chinese practice of copying books was thus an incomparable guarantee of literary culture, and the transcript a key to China's enigmas.

Gloves

In an aversion to animals, the predominant feeling is fear of being recognized by them through contact. The horror that stirs deep in man is an obscure awareness that something living within him is so akin to the disgust-arousing animal that it might be recognized. All disgust is originally disgust at touching. Even when the feeling is mastered, it is only by a drastic gesture that overleaps its mark: the nauseating is violently engulfed, eaten, while the zone of finest epidermal contact remains taboo. Only in this way is the paradox of the moral demand to be met, exacting simultaneously the overcoming and the subtlest elaboration of man's sense of disgust. He may not deny his bestial relationship with the creature, the invocation of which revolts him: he must make himself its master.

Mexican Embassy

Je ne passe jamais devant un fétiche de bois, un Bouddha doré,
une idole mexicaine sans me dire: c'est peut-être le vrai dieu.
[I never pass by a wooden fetish, a gilded Buddha, a Mexican
idol without reflecting: perhaps it is the true God.]
—Charles Baudelaire

I dreamed I was a member of an exploring party in Mexico.
After crossing a high, primeval jungle, we came upon a
system of above-ground caves in the mountains. Here, a reli-
gious order had survived from the time of the first mission-
aries till now, its monks continuing the work of conversion
among the natives. In an immense central grotto with a goth-
ically pointed roof, Mass was celebrated according to the
most ancient rites. We joined the ceremony and witnessed its
climax: toward a wooden bust of God the Father, fixed high
on a wall of the cave, a priest raised a Mexican fetish. At this,
the divine head turned thrice in denial from right to left.

To the Public: Please Protect and Preserve These New Plantings

What is "solved"? Do not all the questions of our lives, as we
live, remain behind us like foliage obstructing our view? To
uproot this foliage, even to thin it out, does not occur to us.
We stride on, leave it behind, and from a distance it is indeed open to view, but indistinct, shadowy, and all the more
enigmatically entangled.

Commentary and translation stand in the same relation to the text as style and mimesis to nature: the same phenomenon considered from different aspects. On the tree of the sacred text, both are only the eternally rustling leaves; on that of the profane, the seasonally falling fruits.

He who loves is attached not only to the "faults" of the beloved, not only to the whims and weaknesses of a woman. Wrinkles in the face, moles, shabby clothes, and a lopsided walk bind him more lastingly and relentlessly than any beauty. This has long been known. And why? If the theory is correct that feeling is not located in the head, that we sentiently experience a window, a cloud, a tree not in our brains but rather in the place where we see it, then we are, in looking at our beloved, too, outside ourselves. But in a torment of tension and ravishment. Our feeling, dazzled, flutters like a flock of birds in the woman's radiance. And as birds seek refuge in the leafy recesses of a tree, feelings escape into the shaded wrinkles, the awkward movements and inconspicuous blemishes of the body we love, where they can lie low in safety. And no passer-by would guess that it is just here, in what is defective and censurable, that the fleeting darts of adoration nestle.

Construction Site

It is folly to brood pedantically over the production of objects—visual aids, toys, or books—that are supposed to be suitable for children. Since the Enlightenment, this has been one of the mustiest speculations of the pedagogues.

Their infatuation with psychology keeps them from perceiving that the world is full of the most unrivaled objects for children's attention and use. And the most specific. For children are particularly fond of haunting any site where things are being visibly worked on. They are irresistibly drawn by the detritus generated by building, gardening, housework, tailoring, or carpentry. In waste products they recognize the face that the world of things turns directly and solely to them. In using these things, they do not so much imitate the works of adults as bring together, in the artifact produced in play, materials of widely differing kinds in a new, intuitive relationship. Children thus produce their own small world of things within the greater one. The norms of this small world must be kept in mind if one wishes to create things specially for children, rather than let one's adult activity, through its requisites and instruments, find its own way to them.

Ministry of the Interior

The more antagonistic a person is toward the traditional order, the more inexorably he will subject his private life to the norms that he wishes to elevate as legislators of a future society. It is as if these laws, nowhere yet realized, placed him under obligation to enact them in advance, at least in the confines of his own existence. In contrast, the man who knows himself to be in accord with the most ancient heritage of his class or nation will sometimes bring his private life into ostentatious contrast to the maxims that he unrelentingly asserts in public, secretly approving his own behavior, without the slightest qualms, as the most conclusive proof of the unshakable authority of the principles he puts on display. Thus are distinguished the types of the anarcho-socialist and the conservative politician.

Flag . . .

How much more easily the leave-taker is loved! For the flame burns more purely for those vanishing in the distance, fueled by the fleeting scrap of material waving from the ship or railway window. Separation penetrates the disappearing person like a pigment and steeps him in gentle radiance.

. . . at Half-Mast

When a person very close to us is dying, there is (we dimly apprehend) something in the months to come that—much as we should have liked to share it with him—could happen only through his absence. We greet him, at the last, in a language that he already no longer understands.

Imperial Panorama[5]

A TOUR THROUGH THE GERMAN INFLATION[6]

I. In the stock of phraseology that lays bare the amalgam of stupidity and cowardice constituting the mode of life of the German bourgeois, the locution referring to impending catastrophe—"Things can't go on like this"—is particularly noteworthy. The helpless fixation on notions of security and property deriving from past decades keeps the average citizen from perceiving the quite remarkable stabilities of an entirely new kind that underlie the present situation. Because the relative stabilization of the prewar years benefited him, he feels compelled to regard any state that dispossesses him as unstable. But stable conditions need by no means be pleasant conditions, and even before the war there were strata for whom stabilized conditions were stabilized wretchedness. To decline is no less stable, no more surprising, than to rise. Only a view that acknowledges downfall as the sole reason for the present situation can advance beyond enervating amazement at what is daily repeated, and perceive the phenomena of decline as stability itself and rescue alone as extraordinary, verging on the marvelous and incomprehensible. People in the national communities of Central Europe live like the inhabitants of an encircled town whose provisions and gunpowder are running out and for whom deliverance is, by human reasoning, scarcely to be expected—a situation in which surrender, perhaps unconditional, should be most seriously considered. But the silent, invisible power that Central Europe feels opposing it does not negotiate. Nothing, therefore, remains but to direct the gaze, in perpetual expectation of the final onslaught, on nothing except the extraordinary event in which alone salvation now lies. But this necessary state of intense and uncomplaining attention could, because we are in mysterious contact with the powers besieging us, really call forth a miracle. Conversely, the assumption that things cannot go on like this will one day confront the fact that for the suffering of individuals, as of communities, there is only one limit beyond which things cannot go: annihilation.

II. A curious paradox: people have only the narrowest private interest in mind when they act, yet they are at the same time more than ever determined in their behavior by the instincts of the mass. And mass instincts have become confused and estranged from life more than ever. Whereas the obscure impulse of the animal (as innumerable anecdotes relate) detects, as danger approaches, a way of escape that still seems invisible, this society, each of whose members cares only for his own abject well-being, falls victim— with animal insensibility but without the insensate intuition of animals—as a blind mass, to even the most obvious danger, and the diversity of individual goals is immaterial in face of the identity of the determining forces. Again and again it has been shown that society's attachment to its familiar and long-since-forfeited life is so rigid as to nullify the genuinely human application of intellect, forethought, even in dire peril. So that in this society the picture of imbecility is complete: uncertainty, indeed perversion, of vital instincts; and impotence, indeed decay, of the intellect. This is the condition of the entire German bourgeoisie.

III. All close relationships are lit up by an almost intolerable, piercing clarity in which they are scarcely able to survive. For on the one hand, money stands ruinously at the center of every vital interest, but, on the other, this is the very barrier before which almost all relationships halt; so, more and more, in the natural as in the moral sphere, unreflecting trust, calm, and health are disappearing.

IV. Not without reason is it customary to speak of "naked" misery. What is most damaging in the display of it, a practice started under the dictates of necessity and making visible only a thousandth part of the hidden distress, is not the onlooker's pity or his equally terrible awareness of his own impunity, but his shame. It is impossible to remain in a large German city, where hunger forces the most wretched to live on the banknotes with which passers-by seek to cover an exposure that wounds them.

V. "Poverty disgraces no man." Well and good. But *they* disgrace the poor man. They do it, and then console him with the little adage. It is one of those that may once have been true but have long since degenerated. The case is no different with the brutal dictum, "If a man does not work, neither shall he eat." When there was work that fed a man, there was also poverty that did not disgrace him, if it arose from deformity or other misfortune. But this deprivation, into which millions are born and hundreds of thousands are dragged by impoverishment, does indeed bring disgrace. Filth and misery grow up around them like walls, the work of invisible hands. And just as a man can endure much in isolation but feels justifiable shame when his wife sees him bear it or suffers it herself, so he may tolerate much so long as he is alone, and everything so long as he conceals it. But no one may ever make peace with poverty when it falls like a gigantic shadow upon his countrymen and his house. Then he must be alert to every humiliation done to him, and so discipline himself that his suffering becomes no longer the downhill road of grief but the rising path of revolt. Yet there is no hope of this so long as each blackest, most terrible stroke of fate, daily and even hourly discussed by the press, set forth in all its illusory causes and effects, helps no one uncover the dark powers that hold his life in thrall.

VI. To the foreigner who is cursorily acquainted with the pattern of German life and who has even briefly traveled about the country, its inhabitants seem no less bizarre than an exotic race. A witty Frenchman has said: "A German seldom understands himself. If he has once understood himself, he will not say so. If he says so, he will not make himself understood." This comfortless distance was increased by the war, but not merely through the real and legendary atrocities that Germans are reported to have committed. Rather, what completes the isolation of Germany in the eyes of other Europeans—what really engenders the attitude that, in dealing with the Germans, they are dealing with Hottentots (as it has been aptly put)—is the violence, incomprehensible to outsiders and wholly imperceptible to those imprisoned by it, with which circumstances, squalor, and stupidity here subjugate people entirely to collective forces, as the lives of savages alone are subjected to tribal laws. The most European of all accomplishments, that more or less discernible irony with which the life of the individual asserts the right to run its course independently of the community into which it is cast, has completely deserted the Germans.

VII. The freedom of conversation is being lost. If, earlier, it was a matter of course in conversation to take interest in one's interlocutor, now this is replaced by inquiry into the cost of his shoes or of his umbrella. Irresistibly intruding on any convivial exchange is the theme of the conditions of life, of money. What this theme involves is not so much the concerns and sorrows of individuals, in which they might be able to help one another, as the overall picture. It is as if one were trapped in a theater and had to follow the events on the stage whether one wanted to or not—had to make them again and again, willingly or unwillingly, the subject of one's thought and speech.

VIII. Anyone who does not simply refuse to perceive decline will hasten to claim a special justification for his own continued presence, his activity and involvement in this chaos. There are as many exceptions for one's own sphere of action, place of residence, and moment of time as there are insights into the general failure. A blind determination to save the prestige of personal existence—rather than, through an impartial disdain for its impotence and entanglement, at least to detach it from the background of universal delusion—is triumphing almost everywhere. That is why the air is so thick with life theories and world views, and why in this country they cut so presumptuous a figure, for almost always they finally serve to sanction some utterly trivial private situation. For just the same reason the air is teeming with phantoms, mirages of a glorious cultural future breaking upon us overnight in spite of all, for everyone is committed to the optical illusions of his isolated standpoint.

IX. The people cooped up in this country no longer discern the contours of human personality. Every free man appears to them as an eccentric. Let us imagine the peaks of the High Alps silhouetted not against the sky but against folds of dark drapery. The mighty forms would show up only dimly. In just this way a heavy curtain shuts off Germany's sky, and we no longer see the profiles of even the greatest men.

X. Warmth is ebbing from things. Objects of daily use gently but insistently repel us. Day by day, in overcoming the sum of secret resistances—not only the overt ones—that they put in our way, we have an immense labor to perform. We must compensate for their coldness with our warmth if they are not to freeze us to death, and handle their spiny forms with infinite dexterity if we are not to bleed to death. From our fellow men we should expect no succor. Bus conductors, officials, workmen, salesmen—they all feel themselves to be the representatives of a refractory material world whose menace they take pains to demonstrate through their own surliness. And in the denaturing of things—a denaturing with which, emulating human decay, they punish humanity—the country itself conspires. It gnaws at us like the things, and the German spring that never comes is only one of countless related phenomena of decomposing German nature. Here one lives as if the weight of the column of air that everyone supports had suddenly, against all laws, become in these regions perceptible.

XI. Any human movement, whether it springs from an intellectual or even a natural impulse, is impeded in its unfolding by the boundless resistance of the outside world.

A shortage of houses and the rising cost of travel are in the process of annihilating the elementary symbol of European freedom, which existed in certain forms even in the Middle Ages: freedom of domicile. And if medieval coercion bound men to natural associations, they are now chained together in unnatural community. Few things will further the ominous spread of the cult of rambling as much as the strangulation of the freedom of residence, and never has freedom of movement stood in greater disproportion to the abundance of means of travel.

XII. Just as all things, in an irreversible process of mingling and contamination, are losing their intrinsic character while ambiguity displaces authenticity, so is the city. Great cities—whose incomparably sustaining and reassuring power encloses those who work within them in an internal truce [*Burgfrieden*] and lifts from them, with the view of the horizon, awareness of the ever-vigilant elemental forces—are seen to be breached at all points by the invading countryside. Not by the landscape, but by what is bitterest in untrammeled nature: ploughed land, highways, night sky that the veil of vibrant redness no longer conceals. The insecurity of even the busy areas puts the city dweller in the opaque and truly dreadful situation in which he must assimilate, along with isolated monstrosities from the open country, the abortions of urban architectonics.

XIII. Noble indifference to the spheres of wealth and poverty has quite forsaken manufactured things. Each thing stamps its owner, leaving him only the choice of appearing a starveling or a racketeer. For although even true luxury can be permeated by intellect and conviviality and so forgotten, the luxury goods swaggering before us now parade such brazen solidity that all the mind's shafts break harmlessly on their surface.

XIV. The earliest customs of peoples seem to send us a warning that, in accepting what we receive so abundantly from nature, we should guard against a gesture of avarice. For we are unable to make Mother Earth any gift of our own. It is therefore fitting to show respect in taking, by returning a part of all we receive before laying hands on our share. This respect is expressed in the ancient custom of the libation. Indeed, it is perhaps this immemorial practice that has survived, transformed, in the prohibition on gathering forgotten ears of corn or fallen grapes, these reverting to the soil or to the ancestral dispensers of blessings. An Athenian custom forbade the picking up of crumbs at the table, since they belonged to the heroes.—If society has so denatured itself through necessity and greed that it can now receive the gifts of nature only rapaciously—that it snatches the fruit unripe from the trees in order to sell it most profitably, and is compelled to empty each dish in its determination to have enough—the earth will be impoverished and the land will yield bad harvests.

Underground Works

In a dream, I saw barren terrain. It was the marketplace at Weimar. Excavations were in progress. I, too, scraped about in the sand. Then the tip of a church steeple came to light.

Delighted, I thought to myself: a Mexican shrine from the time of pre-animism, from the Anaquivitzli. I awoke laughing. (*Ana* = ἀνά; *vi* = *vie*; *witz* [joke] = Mexican church [!])

Coiffeur for Easily Embarrassed Ladies

Three thousand ladies and gentlemen from the Kurfürsten-damm are to be arrested in their beds one morning without explanation and detained for twenty-four hours. At midnight a questionnaire on the death penalty is distributed to the cells—a questionnaire requiring its signatories to indicate which form of execution they would prefer, should the occasion arise. Those who hitherto had merely offered their unsolicited views "in all conscience" would have to complete this document "to the best of their knowledge." By first light—the hour that in olden times was held sacred but that in this country is dedicated to the executioner—the question of capital punishment would be resolved.

Caution: Steps

Work on good prose has three steps: a musical stage when it is composed, an architectonic one when it is built, and a textile one when it is woven.

Attested Auditor of Books

Just as this era is the antithesis of the Renaissance in general, it contrasts in particular with the situation in which the art of printing was discovered. For whether by coincidence or not, printing appeared in Germany at a time when the book in the most eminent sense of the word—the Book of Books—had, through Luther's translation, become the people's property. Now everything indicates that the book in this traditional form is nearing its end. Mallarmé, who in the crystalline structure of his manifestly traditionalist writing saw the true image of what was to come, was in the *Coup de dés* the first to incorporate the graphic tensions of the advertisement in the printed page. The typographic experiments later undertaken by the Dadaists stemmed, it is true, not from constructive principles but from the precise nervous reactions of these literati, and were therefore far less enduring than Mallarmé's, which grew out of the inner nature of his style. But for this very reason they show the contemporary relevance of what Mallarmé, monadically, in his hermetic room, had discovered through a preestablished harmony with all the decisive events of our times in economics, technology, and public life. Script—having found, in the book, a refuge in which it can lead an autonomous existence—is pitilessly dragged out into the street by advertisements and subjected to the brutal heteronomies of economic chaos. This is the hard schooling of its new form. If centuries ago it began gradually to lie down, passing from the upright inscription to the manuscript resting on sloping desks before finally taking itself to bed in the printed book, it now begins just as slowly to rise again from the ground. The newspaper is read more in the vertical than in the horizontal plane, while film and advertisement force the printed word entirely into the dictatorial perpendicular. And before a contemporary finds his way clear to opening a book, his eyes have been exposed to such a blizzard of changing, colorful, conflicting letters that the chances of his penetrating the archaic stillness of the book are slight. Locust swarms of print, which already eclipse the sun of what city dwellers take for intellect, will grow thicker with each succeeding year. Other demands of business life lead further. The card index marks the conquest of three-dimensional writing, and so presents an astonishing counterpoint to the three-dimensionality of script in its original form as rune or knot notation. (And today the book is already, as the present mode of scholarly production demonstrates, an outdated mediation between two different filing systems. For everything that matters is to be found in the card box of the researcher who wrote it, and the scholar studying it assimilates it into his own card index.) But it is quite beyond doubt that the development of writing will not indefinitely be bound by the claims to power of a chaotic academic and commercial activity; rather, quantity is approaching the moment of a qualitative leap when writing, advancing ever more deeply into the graphic regions of its new eccentric figurativeness, will suddenly take possession of an adequate material content. In this picture-writing, poets, who will now as in earliest times be first and foremost experts in writing, will be able to participate only by mastering the fields in which (quite unobtrusively) it is being constructed: statistical and technical diagrams. With the founding of an international moving script, poets will renew their authority in the life of peoples, and find a role awaiting them in comparison to which all the innovative aspirations of rhetoric will reveal themselves as antiquated daydreams.

Teaching Aid

PRINCIPLES OF THE WEIGHTY TOME, OR HOW TO WRITE FAT BOOKS

I. The whole composition must be permeated with a protracted and wordy exposition of the initial plan.

II. Terms are to be included for conceptions that, except in this definition, appear nowhere in the whole book.

III. Conceptual distinctions laboriously arrived at in the text are to be obliterated again in the relevant notes.

IV. For concepts treated only in their general significance, examples should be given; if, for example, machines are mentioned, all the different kinds of machines should be enumerated.

V. Everything that is known a priori about an object is to be consolidated by an abundance of examples.

VI. Relationships that could be represented graphically must be expounded in words. Instead of being represented in a genealogical tree, for example, all family relationships are to be enumerated and described.

VII. Numerous opponents who all share the same argument should each be refuted individually.

The typical work of modern scholarship is intended to be read like a catalogue. But when shall we actually write books like catalogues? If the deficient content were thus to determine the outward form, an excellent piece of writing would result, in which the value of opinions would be marked without their being thereby put on sale.

The typewriter will alienate the hand of the man of letters from the pen only when the precision of typographic forms has directly entered the conception of his books. One might suppose that new systems with more variable type-faces would then be needed. They will replace the pliancy of the hand with the innervation of commanding fingers.

A period that, constructed metrically, afterward has its rhythm upset at a single point yields the finest prose sentence imaginable. In this way a ray of light falls through a chink in the wall of the alchemist's cell, to light up gleaming crystals, spheres, and triangles.

Germans, Drink German Beer!

The mob, impelled by a frenetic hatred of the life of the mind, has found a sure way to annihilate it in the counting of bodies. Given the slightest opportunity, they form ranks and advance into artillery barrages and department stores in marching order. No one sees further than the back before him, and each is proud to be thus exemplary for the eyes behind. Men have been adept at this for centuries in the field, but the parade-march of penury, standing in line, is the invention of women.

Post No Bills

THE WRITER'S TECHNIQUE IN THIRTEEN THESES

I. Anyone intending to embark on a major work should be lenient with himself and, having completed a stint, deny himself nothing that will not prejudice the next.

II. Talk about what you have written, by all means, but do not read from it while the work is in progress. Every gratification procured in this way will slacken your tempo. If this regime is followed, the growing desire to communicate will become in the end a motor for completion.

III. In your working conditions, avoid everyday mediocrity. Semi-relaxation, to a background of insipid sounds, is degrading. On the other hand, accompaniment by an étude or a cacophony of voices can become as significant for work as the perceptible silence of the night. If the latter sharpens the inner ear, the former acts as touchstone for a diction ample enough to bury even the most wayward sounds.

IV. Avoid haphazard writing materials. A pedantic adherence to certain papers, pens, inks is beneficial. No luxury, but an abundance of these utensils is indispensable.

V. Let no thought pass incognito, and keep your notebook as strictly as the authorities keep their register of aliens.

VI. Keep your pen aloof from inspiration, which it will then attract with magnetic power. The more circumspectly you delay writing down an idea, the more maturely developed it will be on surrendering itself. Speech conquers thought, but writing commands it.

VII. Never stop writing because you have run out of ideas. Literary honor requires that one break off only at an appointed moment (a mealtime, a meeting) or at the end of the work.

VIII. Fill the lacunae in your inspiration by tidily copying out what you have already written. Intuition will awaken in the process.

IX. *Nulla dies sine linea*[7]—but there may well be weeks.

X. Consider no work perfect over which you have not once sat from evening to broad daylight.

XI. Do not write the conclusion of a work in your familiar study. You would not find the necessary courage there.

XII. Stages of composition: idea—style—writing. The value of the fair copy is that in producing it you confine attention to calligraphy. The idea kills inspiration; style fetters the idea; writing pays off style.

XIII. The work is the death mask of its conception.

THIRTEEN THESES AGAINST SNOBS

(Snob in the private office of art criticism. On the left, a child's drawing; on the right, a fetish. Snob: "Picasso might as well pack it in!")

I.	The artist makes a work.	The primitive man expresses himself in documents.
II.	The artwork is only incidentally a document.	No document is, as such, a work of art.
III.	The artwork is a masterpiece.	The document serves to instruct.
IV.	With artworks, artists learn their craft.	With documents, a public is educated.
V.	Artworks are remote from one another in their perfection.	All documents communicate through their subject matter.
VI.	In the artwork, content and form are one: meaning [*Gehalt*].	In documents the subject matter is wholly dominant.
VII.	Meaning is the outcome of experience.	Subject matter is the outcome of dreams.
VIII.	In the artwork, subject matter is ballast jettisoned by contemplation.	The more one loses oneself in a document, the denser the subject matter grows.
IX.	In the artwork, the formal law is central.	Forms are merely dispersed in documents.
X.	The artwork is synthetic: an energy-center.	The fertility of the document demands: analysis.

XI. The artwork intensifies itself under the repeated gaze.	A document overpowers only through surprise.
XII. The masculinity of works lies in assault.	The document's innocence gives it cover.
XIII. The artist sets out to conquer meanings.	The primitive man barricades himself behind subject matter.

THE CRITIC'S TECHNIQUE IN THIRTEEN THESES

I. The critic is the strategist in the literary struggle.

II. He who cannot take sides must keep silent.

III. The critic has nothing in common with the interpreter of past cultural epochs.

IV. Criticism must speak the language of artists. For the concepts of the *cénacle* are slogans. And only in slogans is the battle-cry heard.

V. "Objectivity" must always be sacrificed to partisanship, if the cause fought for merits this.

VI. Criticism is a moral question. If Goethe misjudged Hölderlin and Kleist, Beethoven and Jean Paul,[8] his morality and not his artistic discernment was at fault.

VII. For the critic, his colleagues are the higher authority. Not the public. Still less, posterity.

VIII. Posterity forgets or acclaims. Only the critic judges in the presence of the author.

IX. Polemics mean to destroy a book using a few of its sentences. The less it has been studied, the better. Only he who can destroy can criticize.

X. Genuine polemics approach a book as lovingly as a cannibal spices a baby.

XI. Artistic enthusiasm is alien to the critic. In his hand, the artwork is the shining sword in the battle of minds.

XII. The art of the critic in a nutshell: to coin slogans without betraying ideas. The slogans of an inadequate criticism peddle ideas to fashion.

XIII. The public must always be proved wrong, yet always feel represented by the critic.

Number 13

Treize—j'eus un plaisir cruel de m'arrêter sur ce nombre.
[Thirteen—stopping at this number, I felt a cruel pleasure.]
—Marcel Proust

Le reploiement vierge du livre, encore, prête à un sacrifice dont saigna la tranche rouge des anciens tomes; l'introduction d'une arme, ou coupe-papier, pour établir la prise de possession.
[The tight-folded book, virginal still, awaiting the sacrifice that bloodied the red edges of earlier volumes; the insertion of a weapon, or paper-knife, to effect the taking of possession.]
—Stéphane Mallarmé

I. Books and harlots can be taken to bed.

II. Books and harlots interweave time. They command night as day, and day as night.

III. No one can tell from looking at books and harlots that minutes are precious to them. But closer acquaintance shows what a hurry they are in. As our interest becomes absorbed, they, too, are counting.

IV. Books and harlots have always been unhappily in love with each other.

V. Books and harlots: both have their type of man, who lives off them as well as harasses them. In the case of books, critics.

VI. Books and harlots in public establishments—for students.

VII. Books and harlots: seldom does one who has possessed them witness their end. They are apt to vanish before they expire.

VIII. Books and harlots are fond of recounting, mendaciously, how they became what they are. In reality, they did not often notice it themselves. For years one follows "the heart" wherever it leads, and one day a corpulent body stands soliciting on the spot where one had lingered merely to "study life."

IX. Books and harlots love to turn their backs when putting themselves on show.

X. Books and harlots have a large progeny.

XI. Books and harlots: "Old hypocrites—young whores." How many books that were once notorious now serve as instruction for youth!

XII. Books and harlots have their quarrels in public.

XIII. Books and harlots: footnotes in one are as banknotes in the stockings of the other.

Ordnance

I had arrived in Riga to visit a woman friend. Her house,
the town, the language were unfamiliar to me. Nobody was
expecting me; no one knew me. For two hours I walked the
streets in solitude. Never again have I seen them so. From
every gate a flame darted; each cornerstone sprayed sparks,
and every streetcar came toward me like a fire engine. For
she might have stepped out of the gateway, around the
corner, been sitting in the streetcar. But of the two of us, I
had to be, at any price, the first to see the other. For had she
touched me with the match of her eyes, I would have gone
up like a powder keg.

First Aid

A highly convoluted neighborhood, a network of streets that
I had avoided for years, was disentangled at a single stroke
when one day a person dear to me moved there. It was as if
a searchlight set up at this person's window dissected the
area with pencils of light.

Interior Decoration

The tractatus is an Arabic form. Its exterior is undifferenti-
ated and unobtrusive, like the façades of Arabian buildings,
whose articulation begins only in the courtyard. So, too, the
articulated structure of the tractatus is invisible from the
outside, revealing itself only from within. If it is formed by

chapters, they have not verbal headings but numbers. The surface of its deliberations is not enlivened with pictures, but covered with unbroken, proliferating arabesques. In the ornamental density of this presentation, the distinction between thematic and excursive expositions is abolished.

Stationers

Pharus map.[9]—I know someone who is absent-minded. Whereas the names of my suppliers, the location of my documents, the addresses of my friends and acquaintances, the hour of a rendezvous are at my fingertips, in this person political concepts, party slogans, declarations, and commands are firmly lodged. She lives in a city of watchwords and inhabits a neighborhood of conspiratorial and fraternal terms, where every alleyway shows its color and every word has a password for its echo.

List of wishes.—"Does not the reed the world / With sweetness fill? / May no less gracious word / Flow from my quill!"[10] This follows "Blessed Yearning" ["Selige Sehnsucht"] like a pearl that has rolled from a freshly opened oystershell.

Pocket diary.—Few things are more characteristic of the Nordic man than that, when in love, he must above all and at all costs be alone with himself—must first contemplate, enjoy his feeling in solitude—before going to the woman to declare it.

Paperweight.—Place de la Concorde: the Obelisk. What was carved in it four thousand years ago today stands at the center in the greatest of city squares. Had that been foretold to the Pharaoh, what a feeling of triumph it would given him! The foremost Western cultural empire would one day bear at its center the memorial of his rule. How does this apotheosis appear in reality? Not one among the tens of thousands who pass by pauses; not one among the tens of thousands who pause can read the inscription. In such a way does all fame redeem its pledges, and no oracle can match its guile. For the immortal stands like this obelisk, regulating the spiritual traffic that surges thunderously about him—and the inscription he bears helps no one.

Fancy Goods

The incomparable language of the death's-head: total expressionlessness—the black of the eye sockets—coupled with the most unbridled expression—the grinning rows of teeth.

Someone who, feeling abandoned, takes up a book, finds with a pang that the page he is about to turn is already cut, and that even here he is not needed.

Gifts must affect the receiver to the point of shock.

When a valued, cultured, and elegant friend sent me his new book and I was about to open it, I caught myself in the act of straightening my tie.

He who observes etiquette but objects to lying is like someone who dresses fashionably but wears no shirt.

If the smoke from the tip of my cigarette and the ink from the nib of my pen flowed with equal ease, I would be in the Arcadia of my writing.

To be happy is to be able to become aware of oneself without fright.

Enlargements

Child reading.—You are given a book from the school library. In the lower classes, books are simply handed out. Only now and again do you dare express a desire. Often, in envy, you see coveted books pass into other hands. At last, your wish was granted. For a week you were wholly given up to the soft drift of the text, which surrounded you as secretly, densely, and unceasingly as snow. You entered it with limitless trust. The peacefulness of the book that enticed you further and further! Its contents did not much matter. For you were reading at the time when you still made up stories in bed. The child seeks his way along the half-hidden paths. Reading, he covers his ears; the book is on a table that is far too high, and one hand is always on the page. To him, the hero's adventures can still be read in the swirling letters like figures and messages in drifting snowflakes. His breath is part of the air of the events narrated, and all the participants breathe it. He mingles with the characters far more closely than grown-ups do. He is unspeakably touched by the deeds, the words that are exchanged; and, when he gets up, he is covered over and over by the snow of his reading.

Belated child.—The clock over the school playground seems as if damaged on his account. The hands stand at "Tardy." And as he passes in the corridor, murmurs of secret consultation come from the classroom doors. The teachers and pupils behind them are friends. Or all is silent, as if they were waiting for someone. Inaudibly, he puts his hand to the doorhandle. The spot where he stands is steeped in sunlight. Violating the peaceful hour, he opens the door. The teacher's voice clatters like a mill wheel; he stands before the grinding stones. The voice clatters on without a break, but the mill workers now shake off their load to the newcomer. Ten, twenty heavy sacks fly toward him; these he must carry to the bench. Each thread of his jacket is flour-white. Like the tread of a wretched soul at midnight, his every step makes a clatter, and no one notices. Once arrived at his seat, he works quietly with the rest until the bell sounds. But it avails him nothing.

Pilfering child.—Through the chink of the scarcely open larder door, his hand advances like a lover through the night. Once at home in the darkness, it gropes toward sugar or almonds, raisins or preserves. And just as the lover embraces his girl before kissing her, the child's hand enjoys a tactile tryst with the comestibles before his mouth savors their sweetness. How flatteringly honey, heaps of currants, even rice yield to his hand! How passionate this meeting of two who have at last escaped the spoon! Grateful and tempestuous, like someone who has been abducted from the parental home, strawberry jam, unencumbered by bread rolls, abandons itself to his delectation and, as if under the open sky, even the butter responds tenderly to the boldness of this wooer who has penetrated her boudoir. His hand, the juvenile Don Juan, has soon invaded all the cells and spaces, leaving behind it running layers and streaming plenty: virginity renewing itself without complaint.

Child on the carousel.—The platform bearing the docile animals moves close to the ground. It is at the height which, in dreams, is best for flying. Music starts, and the child moves away from his mother with a jerk. At first he is afraid to leave her. But then he notices how brave he himself is. He is ensconced, like the just ruler, over a world that belongs to him. Tangential trees and natives line his way. Then, in an Orient, his mother reappears. Next, emerging from the jungle, comes a treetop, exactly as the child saw it thousands of years ago—just now on the carousel. His beast is devoted: like a mute Arion he rides his silent fish,[11] or a wooden Zeus-bull carries him off like an immaculate Europa. The eternal recurrence of all things has long become child's wisdom, and life a primeval frenzy of domination, with the booming orchestrion as the crown jewels at the center. As the music slows, space begins to stammer and the trees to come to their senses. The carousel becomes uncertain ground. And his mother appears, the much-hammered stake about which the landing child winds the rope of his gaze.

Untidy child.—Each stone he finds, each flower he picks, and each butterfly he catches is already the start of a collection, and every single thing he owns makes up one great collection. In him this passion shows its true face, the stern Indian expression that lingers on, but with a dimmed and manic glow, in antiquarians, researchers, bibliomaniacs. Scarcely has he entered life than he is a hunter. He hunts the spirits whose trace he scents in things; between spirits and things, years pass in which his field of vision remains free of people. His life is like a dream: he knows nothing lasting;

everything seemingly happens to him by chance. His nomad-years are hours in the forest of dream. To this forest he drags home his booty, to purify it, secure it, cast out its spell. His dresser drawers must become arsenal and zoo, crime museum and crypt. "To tidy up" would be to demolish an edifice full of prickly chestnuts that are spiky clubs, tinfoil that is hoarded silver, bricks that are coffins, cacti that are totem poles, and copper pennies that are shields. The child has long since helped at his mother's linen cupboard and his father's bookshelves, while in his own domain he is still a sporadic, warlike visitor.

Child hiding.—He already knows all the hiding places in the apartment, and returns to them as if to a house where everything is sure to be just as it was. His heart pounds; he holds his breath. Here he is enclosed in the material world. It becomes immensely distinct, speechlessly obtrusive. Only in such a way does a man who is being hanged become aware of the reality of rope and wood. Standing behind the doorway curtain, the child himself becomes something floating and white, a ghost. The dining table under which he is crouching turns him into the wooden idol in a temple whose four pillars are the carved legs. And behind a door, he himself *is* the door—wears it as his heavy mask, and like a shaman will bewitch all those who unsuspectingly enter. At all cost, he must avoid being found. When he makes faces, he is told that all the clock has to do is strike, and his face will stay like that forever. The element of truth in this, he finds out in his hiding place. Anyone who discovers him can petrify him as an idol under the table, weave him forever as a ghost into the curtain, banish him for life into the heavy door. And so, at the seeker's touch, he drives out with a loud cry the demon who has so transformed him; indeed, without waiting for the moment of discovery, he grabs the hunter with a shout of self-deliverance. That is why he does not tire of the struggle with the demon. In this struggle, the apartment is the arsenal of his masks. Yet once each year— in mysterious places, in their empty eye sockets, in their fixed mouths—presents lie. Magical experience becomes science. As its engineer, the child disenchants the gloomy parental apartment and looks for Easter eggs.

Antiques

Medallion.—In everything that is with reason called beautiful, appearance has a paradoxical effect.

Prayer wheel.—Only images in the mind vitalize the will. The mere word, by contrast, at most inflames it, to leave it smouldering, blasted. There is no intact will without exact pictorial imagination. No imagination without inner-vation. Now breathing is the latter's most delicate regulator. The sound of formulas is a canon of such breathing. Hence the practice of yoga meditation, which breathes in accord with the holy syllables. Hence its omnipotence.

Antique spoon.—One thing is reserved to the greatest epic writers: the capacity to feed their heroes.

Old map.—In a love affair, most people seek an eternal homeland. Others, but very few, eternal voyaging. The latter are melancholics, who believe that contact with Mother

Earth is to be shunned. They seek the person who will keep the homeland's sadness far away from them. To that person they remain faithful. The medieval complexion-books understood the yearning of this human type for long journeys.[12]

Fan.—The following experience will be familiar: if one is in love, or just intensely preoccupied with another person, his portrait will appear in almost every book. Moreover, he appears as both protagonist and antagonist. In stories, novels, and novellas, he is encountered in endless metamorphoses. And from this it follows that the faculty of imagination is the gift of interpolating into the infinitely small, of inventing, for every intensity, an extensiveness to contain its new, compressed fullness—in short, of receiving each image as if it were that of the folded fan, which only in spreading draws breath and flourishes, in its new expanse, the beloved features within it.

Relief.—One is with the woman one loves, speaks with her. Then, weeks or months later, separated from her, one thinks again of what was talked of then. And now the motif seems banal, tawdry, shallow, and one realizes that it was she alone, bending low over it with love, who shaded and sheltered it before us, so that the thought was alive in all its folds and crevices like a relief. Alone, as now, we see it lie flat, bereft of comfort and shadow, in the light of our knowledge.

Torso.—Only he who can view his own past as an abortion sprung from compulsion and need can use it to full advantage in every present. For what one has lived is at best comparable to a beautiful statue that has had all its limbs broken off in transit, and that now yields nothing but the precious block out of which the image of one's future must be hewn.

Watchmaker and Jeweler

He who, awake and dressed, perhaps while hiking, witnesses the sunrise, preserves all day before others the serenity of one invisibly crowned, and he who sees daybreak while working feels at midday as if he himself has placed this crown upon his head.

Like a clock of life on which the seconds race, the page number hangs over the characters in a novel. Where is the reader who has not once lifted to it a fleeting, fearful glance?

I dreamed that I was walking—a newly hatched private tutor—conversing collegially with Roethe, through the spacious rooms of a museum where he was the curator.[13] While he talks in an adjoining room with an employee, I go up to a glass display case. In it, next to other, lesser objects, stands a metallic or enameled, dully shining, almost life-size bust of a woman, not unlike Leonardo's Flora in the Berlin Museum. The mouth of this golden head is open, and over the lower teeth jewelry, partly hanging from the mouth, is spread at measured intervals. I was in no doubt that this was a clock.—(Dream motifs: blushing for shame [*Scham-Roethe*]; the morning hour has gold in its mouth [*Morgenstunde hat gold im Munde*, "the early bird catches the worm"]; "*La tête, avec l'amas de sa crinière sombre / Et de ses bijoux précieux, /*

Sur la table de nuit, comme une renoncule, / Repose" [The head, heaped with its dark mane / and its precious jewels, / on the night-table, like a ranunculus, / rests]—Baudelaire.)

Arc Lamp

The only way of knowing a person is to love that person without hope.

Loggia

Geranium.—Two people who are in love are attached above all else to their names.

Carthusian carnation.—To the lover, the loved one appears always as solitary.

Asphodel.—Behind someone who is loved, the abyss of sexuality closes like that of the family.

Cactus bloom.—The truly loving person delights in finding the beloved, arguing, in the wrong.

Forget-me-not.—Memory always sees the loved one smaller.

Foliage plant.—In the event an obstacle prevents union, the fantasy of a contented, shared old age is immediately at hand.

Lost-and-Found Office

Articles lost.—What makes the very first glimpse of a village, a town, in the landscape so incomparable and irretrievable is the rigorous connection between foreground and distance. Habit has not yet done its work. As soon as we begin to find our bearings, the landscape vanishes at a stroke, like the façade of a house as we enter it. It has not yet gained preponderance through a constant exploration that has become habit. Once we begin to find our way about, that earliest picture can never be restored.

Articles found.—The blue distance which never gives way to foreground or dissolves at our approach, which is not revealed spread-eagled and longwinded when reached but only looms more compact and threatening, is the painted distance of a backdrop. It is what gives stage sets their incomparable atmosphere.

Stand for Not More than Three Cabs

I stood for ten minutes waiting for an omnibus. "*L'Intran* . . . *Paris-Soir* . . . *La Liberté*," a newspaper vendor called incessantly in an unvarying tone behind me. "*L'Intran* . . . *Paris-Soir* . . . *La Liberté*"—a three-cornered cell in a hard-labor prison. I saw before me how bleak the corners were.

I saw in a dream "a house of ill-repute." "A hotel in which an animal is spoiled. Practically everyone drinks only spoiled animal-water." I dreamed in these words, and at once woke with a start. Extremely tired, I had thrown myself on my bed in my clothes in the brightly lit room, and had immediately, for a few seconds, fallen asleep.

In tenement blocks, there is a music of such deathly sad wantonness that one cannot believe it is intended for the player: it is music for the furnished rooms, where on Sundays someone sits amid thoughts that are soon garnished with these notes, like a bowl of overripe fruit with withered leaves.

Monument to a Warrior

Karl Kraus. —Nothing more desolating than his acolytes, nothing more godforsaken than his adversaries. No name that would be more fittingly honored by silence. In ancient armor, wrathfully grinning, a Chinese idol, brandishing a drawn sword in each hand, he dances a war-dance before the burial vault of the German language. "Merely one of the epigones that live in the old house of language," he has become the sealer of its tomb. Keeping watch day and night, he endures. No post was ever more loyally held, and none was ever more hopelessly lost. Here stands one who, like a Danaïd, fetches water from the ocean of tears of his contemporaries, and from whose hands the rock which is to bury his enemies rolls like that of Sisyphus. What more helpless than his conversion? What more powerless than his humanity? What more hopeless than his battle with the press? What does he know of the powers that are his true allies? But what vision of the new seers bears comparison with the listening of this shaman, whose utterances even a dead language inspires? Who ever conjured up a spirit as Kraus did in "The Forsaken" ["Die Verlassenen"],[14] as if "Blessed Yearning" ["Selige Sehnsucht"] had never been composed? Helpless as only spirits' voices are when summoned up, a murmur from the chthonic depths of language is the source of his sooth-saying. Every sound is incomparably genuine, but they all leave us bewildered, like messages from the beyond. Blind like the *manes*, language calls him to vengeance, as narrow-minded as spirits that know only the voice of the blood, who care not what havoc they wreak in the realm of the living. But he cannot err. Their commands are infallible. Whoever runs into him is condemned already: in his mouth, the adversary's name itself becomes a judgment. When his lips part, the colorless flame of wit darts forth. And no one who walks the paths of life would come upon him. On an archaic field of honor, a gigantic battleground of bloody labor, he rages before a deserted sepulcher. The honors at his death will be immeasurable, and the last that are bestowed.

Fire Alarm

The notion of the class war can be misleading. It does not refer to a trial of strength to decide the question "Who shall win, who be defeated?" or to a struggle whose outcome is good for the victor and bad for the vanquished. To think in this way is to romanticize and obscure the facts. For whether the bourgeoisie wins or loses the fight, it remains doomed by the inner contradictions that in the course of development will become deadly. The only question is whether its downfall will come through itself or through the proletariat. The continuance or the end of three thousand years of cultural development will be decided by the answer. History knows nothing of the evil infinity contained in the image of the two wrestlers locked in eternal combat. The true politician reckons only in dates. And if the abolition of the bourgeoisie is not completed by an almost calculable moment in economic and technical development (a moment signaled by inflation and poison-gas warfare), all is lost. Before the spark reaches the dynamite, the lighted fuse must be cut. The interventions, dangers, and tempi of politicians are technical—not chivalrous.

Travel Souvenirs

Atrani.[15]—The gently rising, curved baroque staircase leading to the church. The railing behind the church. The litanies of the old women at the "Ave Maria": preparing to die first-class. If you turn around, the church verges like God himself on the sea. Each morning the Christian era crumbles the rock, but between the walls below, the night falls always into the four old Roman quarters. Alleyways like air shafts. A well in the marketplace. In the late afternoon, women around it. Then, in solitude: archaic plashing.

Navy.—The beauty of the tall sailing ships is unique. Not only has their outline remained unchanged for centuries, but they appear in the most immutable landscape: at sea, silhouetted against the horizon.

Versailles façade.—It is as if this château had been forgotten where hundreds of years ago it was placed *Par Ordre du Roi* for only two hours as the movable scenery for a *féerie.*[16] Of its splendor it keeps none for itself, giving it undivided to that royal condition which it concludes. Before this backdrop, it becomes a stage on which the tragedy of absolute monarchy was performed like an allegorical ballet. Yet today it is only the wall in the shade of which one seeks to enjoy the prospect into blue distance created by Le Nôtre.[17]

Heidelberg Castle.—Ruins jutting into the sky can appear doubly beautiful on clear days when, in their windows or above their contours, the gaze meets passing clouds. Through the transient spectacle it opens in the sky, destruction reaffirms the eternity of these ruins.

Seville, Alcazar.—An architecture that follows fantasy's first impulse. It is undetected by practical considerations. These rooms provide only for dreams and festivities—their consummation. Here dance and silence become the leitmotifs, since all human movement is absorbed by the soundless tumult of the ornament.

Marseilles cathedral.—On the sunniest, least frequented square stands the cathedral. This place is deserted, despite the fact that near its feet are La Joliette, the harbor, to the south, and a proletarian district to the north. As a reloading point for intangible, unfathomable goods, the bleak building stands between quay and warehouse. Nearly forty years were spent on it. But when all was complete, in 1893, place and time had conspired victoriously in this monument against its architects and sponsors, and the wealth of the clergy had given rise to a gigantic railway station that could never be opened to traffic. The façade gives an indication of the waiting rooms within, where passengers of the first to fourth classes (though before God they are all equal), wedged among their spiritual possessions as if between suitcases, sit reading hymnbooks that, with their concordances and crossreferences, look very much like international timetables. Extracts from the railway traffic regulations in the form of pastoral letters hang on the walls, tariffs for the discount on special trips in Satan's luxury train are consulted, and cabinets where the long-distance traveler can discreetly wash are kept in readiness as confessionals. This is the Marseilles religion station. Sleeping cars to eternity depart from here at Mass times.

Freiburg minster.—The special sense of a town is formed in part for its inhabitants—and perhaps even in the memory of the traveler who has stayed there—by the timber and intervals with which its tower clocks begin to chime.

Moscow, Saint Basil's.—What the Byzantine Madonna carries on her arm is only a life-size wooden doll. Her expression of pain before a Christ whose childhood remains only suggested, represented, is more intense than any she could display with a realistic image of a boy.

Boscotrecase.[18]—The distinction of the forest of stone-pines: its roof is formed without interlacements.

Naples, Museo Nazionale.—Archaic statues offer in their smiles the consciousness of their bodies to the onlooker, as a child holds out to us freshly picked flowers untied and unarranged; later art laces its expressions more tightly, like the adult who binds the lasting bouquet with cut grasses.

Florence, Baptistery.—On the portal, the *Spes* [Hope] by Andrea de Pisano. Sitting, she helplessly extends her arms toward a fruit that remains beyond her reach. And yet she is winged. Nothing is more true.

Sky.—As I stepped from a house in a dream, the night sky met my eyes. It shed intense radiance. For in this plenitude of stars, the images of the constellations stood sensuously present. A Lion, a Maiden, a Scale and many others shone palely down, dense clusters of stars, upon the earth. No moon was to be seen.

Optician

In summer, fat people are conspicuous; in winter, thin.

In spring, attention is caught, in bright sunshine, by the young foliage; in cold rain, by the still-leafless branches.

After a convivial evening, someone remaining behind can see at a glance what it was like from the disposition of plates and cups, glasses and food.

First principle of wooing: to make oneself sevenfold; to place oneself sevenfold about the woman who is desired.

In the eyes we see people to the lees.

Toys

Cut-out models.—Booths have docked like rocking boats on both sides of the stone jetty on which the people jostle. There are sailing vessels with lofty masts hung with pennants, steamers with smoke rising from their funnels, barges that keep their cargoes long stowed. Among them are ships into which one vanishes; only men are admitted, but through hatchways you can see women's arms, veils, peacock feathers. Elsewhere exotic people stand on the deck, apparently trying to frighten the public away with eccentric music. But with what indifference is it received! You climb up hesitantly, with the broad rolling gait used on ships' gangways, and so long as you are aloft you realize that the whole is cut off from the shore. Those who reemerge from below, taciturn and benumbed, have seen, on red scales where dyed alcohol rises and falls, their own marriage come into being and cease to be; the yellow man who began wooing at the foot of this scale, at the top of it deserted his blue wife. In mirrors they have seen the floor melt away beneath their feet like water, and have stumbled into the open on rolling stairways. The fleet has brought unrest to the neighborhood: the women and girls on board have brazen airs, and everything edible has been taken aboard in the land of idle luxury. One is so totally cut off by the ocean that everything is encountered here as if all at once for the first and the last time. Sea lions, dwarfs, and dogs are preserved as if in an ark. Even the railway has been brought in once and for all, and circulates endlessly through a tunnel. For a few days the neighborhood has become the port of a south-sea island, its inhabitants savages swooning in covetous wonderment before the things that Europe tosses at their feet.

Targets.—The landscapes of shooting-ranges in fairground booths ought to be described collectively as a corpus. There is, for example, a polar waste against which are set bundles of white clay pipes, the targets, radiating like spokes. Behind this, and before an unarticulated strip of woodland, two foresters are painted, while right at the front, like movable scenery, are two sirens with provocative breasts, painted in oil colors. Elsewhere pipes bristle from the hair of women who are seldom painted with skirts, usually in tights. Or they protrude from a fan the women spread in their hands. Moving pipes revolve slowly in the further regions of the clay-pigeon booths. Other stands present theatricals directed by the spectator with his rifle. If he hits the bull's-eye, the performance starts. On one occasion there were thirty-six such boxes, and above the stage of each was written what they held in store: *"Jeanne d'Arc en prison,"* *"L'hospitalité," "Les rues de Paris."* On another booth: *"Exécution capitale."* In front of the closed gate a guillotine, a judge in a black robe, and a priest holding a crucifix. If the shot hits the mark, the gate opens and out comes a board on which the miscreant stands between two policemen. He places his neck automatically under the blade and is decapitated. In the same way: *"Les délices du mariage."* A penurious interior is revealed. The father is seen in the middle of the room; he is holding a child on his knee and, with his free hand, rocking a cradle containing another. *"L'Enfer"*: when its gates part, a devil is seen tormenting a wretched soul. Next to him, another is dragging a priest toward a cauldron in which the damned must stew. *"Le bagne"* ["prison"]: a door with a jailer in front of it. When the target is hit, he pulls a bell-cord. The bell rings, the door opens. Two convicts are seen manhandling a big wheel. They seem to have to turn it. Yet another constellation: a fiddler with his dancing bear. When you shoot successfully, the bow moves.

The bear beats a drum with his paw and lifts one leg. One thinks of the fairy tale of the brave little tailor, and could also imagine Sleeping Beauty awakened with a shot, Snow White freed of the apple by a shot, or Little Red Riding Hood released by a shot. The shot breaks in magically upon the existence of the puppets with that curative power that hews the heads from monsters and reveals them to be princesses. As is the case with the great door without an inscription: if you have hit the mark it opens, and before red plush curtains stands a Moor who seems to bow slightly. He holds a golden bowl before him. On it lie three pieces of fruit. The first opens; a tiny person stands inside it and bows. In the second, two equally diminutive puppets revolve in a dance. (The third did not open.) Below, in front of the table on which the remaining scenery stands, a small horseman with the inscription: *"Route minée"* ["mined road"]. If you hit the bull's-eye, there is a bang and the rider somersaults with his horse, but stays—needless to say—in the saddle.

Stereoscope.—Riga. The daily market, a huddling city of low wooden booths, stretches along the jetty, a broad, dirty stone embankment without warehouse buildings, by the waters of the Dvina. Small steamers, often showing no more than their funnels above the quay wall, have put in at the blackish dwarftown. (The larger ships are moored downstream.) Grimy boards are the clay-gray foundation on which, glowing in the cold air, sparse colors melt. At some corners one can find all year round, alongside huts for fish, meat, boots, and clothes, petty-bourgeois women with the colored paper rods that penetrate as far as the West only at

Christmastime. Like being scolded by the most-loved voice: such are these rods. For a few centimes, multicolored chastising switches. At the end of the jetty, fenced off and only thirty paces from the water, are the red-and-white mounds of the apple market. The apples on sale are packed in straw; those sold lie without straw in the housewives' baskets. A dark-red church rises beyond, outshone in the fresh November air by the cheeks of the apples.—Several shops for boat tackle in small houses near the jetty. Ropes are painted on them. Everywhere you see wares depicted on signboards or on house walls. One shop in the town has cases and belts larger than life on its bare brick walls. A low corner-house with a shop for corsets and millinery is decorated with ladies' faces complete with finery, and severe bodices painted on a yellow-ocher ground. Protruding from it at an angle is a lantern with similar pictures on its glass panes. The whole is like the façade of a fantasy brothel. Another house, likewise not far from the harbor, has sugar sacks and coal in gray-and-black relief on a gray wall. Somewhere else, shoes rain from horns of plenty. Ironmongery is painted in detail—hammers, cogs, pliers, and the tiniest screws on one board that looks like a page from an outmoded child's painting-book. The town is permeated with such pictures. Between them, however, rise tall, desolate, fortress-like buildings evoking all the terrors of czarism.

Not for sale.—A mechanical cabinet at the fair at Lucca. The exhibition is accommodated in a long, symmetrically divided tent. A few steps lead up to it. The signboard shows a table with a few motionless puppets. You enter the tent by the right-hand opening and leave it by the left. In the bright interior, two tables extend toward the back. They touch with their inner edge, so that only a narrow space is left in which to walk round. Both tables are low and glass-covered. On them stand the puppets (twenty to twenty-five centimeters high, on average), while in their lower concealed part the clockwork that drives them ticks audibly. A narrow raised board for children runs along the sides of the tables. There are distorting mirrors on the walls.—Next to the entrance, princely personages are to be seen. Each of them makes a particular gesture: one a spacious, inviting movement with the right or left arm, another a swiveling of his glassy eyes; some roll their eyes and move their arms at the same time. Here stand Franz Joseph, Pius IX, enthroned and flanked by two cardinals, Queen Elena of Italy, the sultaness, Wilhelm I on horseback, a small Napoleon III, and an even smaller Victor Emmanuel as crown prince. Biblical figurines follow, then the Passion. Herod orders the slaughter of the infants with manifold movements of the head. He opens his mouth wide while nodding, extends and lets fall his arm. Two executioners stand before him, one free-wheeling with a cutting sword, a decapitated child under his arm; the other, on the point of stabbing, stands motionless but for his rolling eyes. And two mothers are there: one endlessly and gently shaking her head like a depressive, the other raising her arms slowly, beseechingly.—The nailing to the Cross. It lies on the ground. The hirelings hammer in the nails. Christ nods.—Christ crucified, slaked by the vinegar-soaked sponge, which a soldier offers him in slow jerks and then instantly withdraws. Each time, the Savior slightly raises his chin. From behind, an angel bends over the Cross with a chalice for blood, holds it in front of the body and then, as if it were filled, removes it.—The other table shows genre pictures. Gargantua with dumplings. A plateful in front of him, he shovels them into his mouth with both hands, alternately lifting his left arm and his right. Each hand holds a fork on which a dumpling is impaled.—An Alpine maiden spinning.—Two monkeys playing violins.—A magician has two barrel-like containers in front of him. The one on the right opens, and the top half of a lady's body emerges. The one on the left opens: from it rises half-length a man's body. Again the right-hand container opens and now a ram's skull appears with the lady's face between its horns. Then, on the left, a monkey presents itself instead of the man. Then it all starts again from the beginning.—Another magician: he has a table in front of him on which he holds beakers upside-down in each hand. Under them, as he alternately lifts one and then the other, appears now a loaf or an apple, now a flower or dice.—The magic well: a farm boy stands at a well, shaking his head. A girl draws water, and the unfaltering thick stream of glass runs from the well-mouth.—The enchanted lovers: a golden bush or a golden flame parts in two wings. Within are seen two puppets. They turn their faces toward each other and then away, as if looking at each other in confused astonishment.—Below each figure a small label. The whole dating back to 1862.

Polyclinic

The author lays the idea on the marble table of the café. Lengthy observation, for he makes use of the time before the arrival of his glass, the lens through which he examines the patient. Then, deliberately, he unpacks his instruments: fountain pens, pencil, and pipe. The numerous clientele, arranged as in an amphitheater, make up his clinical audience. Coffee, carefully poured and consumed, puts the idea under chloroform. What this idea may be has no more connection with the matter at hand than the dream of an anaesthetized patient has with the surgical intervention. With the cautious lineaments of handwriting, the operator makes incisions, displaces internal accents, cauterizes proliferations of words, inserts a foreign term as a silver rib. At last, the whole is finely stitched together with punctuation, and he pays the waiter, his assistant, in cash.

These Spaces for Rent

Fools lament the decay of criticism. For its day is long past. Criticism is a matter of correct distancing. It was at home in a world where perspectives and prospects counted and where it was still possible to adopt a standpoint. Now things press too urgently on human society. The "unclouded," "innocent" eye has become a lie, perhaps the whole naive mode of expression sheer incompetence. Today the most real, mercantile gaze into the heart of things is the advertisement. It tears down the stage upon which contemplation moved, and all but hits us between the eyes with things as a car, growing to gigantic proportions, careens at us out of a film screen. And just as the film does not present furniture and façades in completed forms for critical inspection, their insistent, jerky nearness alone being sensational, the genuine advertisement hurls things at us with the tempo of a good film. Thereby "matter-of-factness" is finally dispatched, and in the face of the huge images spread across the walls of houses, where toothpaste and cosmetics lie handy for giants, sentimentality is restored to health and liberated in American style, just as people whom nothing moves or touches any longer are taught to cry again by films. For the man in the street, however, it is money that affects him in this way, brings him into perceived contact with things. And the paid reviewer, manipulating paintings in the dealer's exhibition room, knows more important if not better things about them than the art lover viewing them in the gallery window. The warmth of the subject is communicated to him, stirs sentient springs. What, in the end, makes advertisements so superior to criticism? Not what the moving red neon sign says—but the fiery pool reflecting it in the asphalt.

Office Equipment

The boss's room bristles with weapons. The apparent comfort that disarms those entering is in reality a hidden arsenal. A telephone on the desk shrills at every moment. It interrupts you at the most important point and gives your opponent time to contrive an answer. Meanwhile, snatches of conversation show how many matters are dealt with here that are more important than the one under discussion. You say this to yourself, and slowly begin to retreat from your standpoint. You begin to wonder who it is they are talking about, and hear with fright that your interlocutor is leaving tomorrow for Brazil; soon you feel such solidarity with the firm that when he complains of a migraine on the telephone, you regret it as a disturbance of business (rather than welcoming it as an opportunity). Summoned or unsummoned, the secretary enters. She is very pretty. And whether her employer is either indifferent to her charms or has long clarified his position as her admirer, the newcomer will glance over at her more than once; and she knows how to turn this to advantage with her boss. His personnel are in motion, producing card-indexes in which the visitor knows himself to be entered under various rubrics. He starts to tire. The other, with the light behind him, reads this off the dazzlingly illuminated face with satisfaction. The armchair, too, does its work; you sit in it tilted as far back as at the dentist's, and so finally accept this discomfiting procedure as the legitimate state of affairs. This treatment, too, is followed sooner or later by a liquidation.

Mixed Cargo: Shipping and Packing

In the early morning I drove through Marseilles to the station, and as I passed familiar places on my way, and then new, unfamiliar ones or others that I remembered only vaguely, the city became a book in my hands, into which I hurriedly glanced a few last times before it passed from my sight for who knows how long into a warehouse crate.

Closed for Alterations

In a dream, I took my life with a gun. When it went off, I did not wake up but saw myself lying for a while as a corpse. Only then did I wake.

AUGEAS SELF-SERVICE RESTAURANT[19]

This is the weightiest objection to the mode of life of the confirmed bachelor: he eats by himself. Taking food alone tends to make one hard and coarse. Those accustomed to it must lead a spartan life if they are not to go downhill. Hermits have observed, if for only this reason, a frugal diet. For it is only in company that eating is done justice; food must be divided and distributed if it is to be well received. No matter by whom: formerly, a beggar at the table enriched each banquet. The splitting up and giving are all-important, not sociable conversation. What is surprising, on the other hand, is that without food conviviality grows precarious. Playing host levels differences, binds together. The count of Saint-Germain fasted before loaded tables, and by this alone dominated conversation. When all abstain, however, rivalries and conflict ensue.

Stamp Shop

To someone looking through piles of old letters, a stamp that has long been out of circulation on a torn envelope often says more than a reading of dozens of pages. Sometimes you come across stamps on postcards and are unsure whether you should detach them or keep the card as it is, like a page by an old master that has different but equally precious drawings on both sides. There are also, in the glass cases of cafés, letters with insufficient postage, pilloried before all eyes. Or have they been deported, and forced to wait in this case for years, languishing on a glass Salas y Gomez?[20] Letters that remain long unopened take on a brutal look; they are disinherited, and malignantly plot revenge for long days of suffering. Many of them later figure in the windows of stamp dealers, as entires branded over and over with postmarks.

As is known, there are collectors who concern themselves only with postmarked stamps, and it would not be difficult to believe them the only ones who have penetrated the secret. They confine themselves to the occult part of the stamp: the postmark. For the postmark is the night side of stamps. There are ceremonious ones that place a halo about the head of Queen Victoria, and prophetic ones that give Humbert[21] a martyr's crown. But no sadistic fantasy can equal the black practice that covers faces with weals, and cleaves the land of entire continents like an earthquake. And the perverse pleasure in contrasting this violated stamp-body with its white lace-trimmed tulle dress: the serrated border. The pursuer of postmarks must, like a detective, possess information on the most notorious post offices, like an archaeologist the art of reconstructing the torsos of the most foreign place-names, and like a cabbalist an inventory of dates for an entire century.

Stamps bristle with tiny numbers, minute letters, diminutive leaves and eyes. They are graphic cellular tissue.

All this swarms about and, like lower animals, lives on even when mutilated. This is why such powerful pictures can be made of pieces of stamps stuck together. But in them, life always bears a hint of corruption to signify that it is composed of dead matter. Their portraits and obscene groups are littered with bones and riddled with worms.

Do the color sequences of the long sets perhaps refract the light of a strange sun? Did the postal ministries of the Vatican or Ecuador capture rays unknown to us? And why are we not shown the stamps of the superior planets? The thousand gradations of fire-red that are in circulation on Venus, and the four great gray shades of Mars, and the un-numbered stamps of Saturn?

On stamps, countries and oceans are merely the provinces and kings merely the hirelings of numbers that steep them in their colors at will. Stamp albums are magical reference books; the numbers of monarchs and palaces, of animals and allegories and states, are recorded in them. Postal traffic depends on their harmony as the motions of the planets depend on the harmony of the celestial numbers.

Old *groschen*-stamps showing only one or two large figures in an oval. They look like those first photos from which, in blacklacquered frames, relatives we never knew look down on us: figure-shaped great-aunts or forefathers. Thurn und Taxis, too, has the big figures on its stamps; there, they are like the bewitched numbers of taxi meters.[22] One would not be surprised, one evening, to see the light of a candle shining through them from behind. But then there are small stamps without perforations, without any indication of currency or country. In a tightly woven spider's web, they bear only a number. These things are perhaps truly without a fate.

Script on Turkish piaster-stamps is like the slanted, altogether too dandyish, too gleaming breast-pin in the tie of a sly, only half-Europeanized merchant from Constantinople. They number among the postal parvenus, the large, badly perforated, garish formats of Nicaragua or Colombia, which deck themselves out like banknotes.

Extra-postage stamps are the spirits among stamps. They are unaltering. The changes of monarchs and forms of government pass over them without trace, as if over phantoms.

The child looks toward far-off Liberia through an inverted opera-glass: there it lies behind its little strip of sea with its palms, just as the stamps show it. With Vasco da Gama, he sails around a triangle which is as isoscelean as hope and whose colors change with the weather. A travel brochure for the Cape of Good Hope. When he sees the swan on Australian stamps, it is always, even on the blue, green, and brown issues, the black swan that is found only in Australia and that here glides on the waters of a pool as on the most pacific ocean. Stamps are the visiting-cards that the great states leave in a child's room.

Like Gulliver, the child travels among the lands and peoples of his postage stamps. The geography and history of the Lilliputians, the whole science of the little nation with all its figures and names, is instilled in him in sleep. He takes part in their transactions, attends their purple assemblies, watches the launching of their little ships, and celebrates with their crowned heads, enthroned behind hedges, jubilees.

There is, it is known, a stamp-language that is to flower-language what the Morse alphabet is to the written one. But how long will the flowers continue to bloom between the telegraph poles? Are not the great artistic stamps of the postwar years, with their full colors, already the autumnal asters and dahlias of this flora? Stephan, a German and not by chance a contemporary of Jean Paul, planted this seed in the summery middle of the nineteenth century.[23] It will not survive the twentieth.

Si Parla Italiano

I sat at night in violent pain on a bench. Opposite me on another, two girls sat down. They seemed to want to discuss something in confidence and began to whisper. Nobody except me was nearby, and I would not have understood their Italian however loud it had been. But now I could not resist the feeling, in face of this unmotivated whispering in a language inaccessible to me, that a cool dressing was being applied to the painful place.

Technical Aid

Nothing is poorer than a truth expressed as it was thought. Committed to writing in such a case, it is not even a bad photograph. And the truth refuses (like a child or a woman who does not love us), facing the lens of writing while we crouch under the black cloth, to keep still and look amiable. Truth wants to be startled abruptly, at one stroke, from her self-immersion, whether by uproar, music, or cries for help. Who could count the alarm signals with which the inner world of the true writer is equipped? And to "write" is nothing other than to set them jangling. Then the sweet odalisque rises with a start, snatches whatever first comes to hand in the *mêlée* of her boudoir (our cranium), wraps it around her, and—almost unrecognizable—flees from us to other people. But how well-constituted she must be, how healthily built, to step in such a way among them, contorted, rattled, and yet victorious, captivating!

Hardware

Quotations in my work are like wayside robbers who leap out, armed, and relieve the idle stroller of his conviction.

The killing of a criminal can be moral—but never its legitimation.

The provider for all mankind is God, and the state his deputy.

The expressions of people moving about a picture gallery show ill-concealed disappointment that only pictures hang there.

Tax Advice

Beyond doubt: a secret connection exists between the measure of goods and the measure of life—which is to say, between money and time. The more trivial the content of a lifetime, the more fragmented, multifarious, and disparate are its moments, while the grand period characterizes a superior existence. Very aptly, Lichtenberg suggests that time whiled away should be seen as made smaller, rather than shorter, and he also observes: "A few dozen million minutes make up a life of forty-five years and a bit more."[24] When a currency in use is worth so little that a few million units of it are insignificant, life will have to be counted in seconds, rather than years, if it is to appear a respectable sum. And it will be frittered away like a bundle of banknotes: Austria cannot break the habit of thinking in florins.

Money and rain belong together. The weather itself is an index of the state of this world. Bliss is cloudless, knows no weather. There also comes a cloudless realm of perfect goods, on which no money falls.

A descriptive analysis of banknotes is needed. The unlimited satirical force of such a book would be equaled only by its objectivity. For nowhere more naively than in these documents does capitalism display itself in solemn earnest. The innocent cupids frolicking about numbers, the goddesses holding tablets of the law, the stalwart heroes sheathing their swords before monetary units, are a world of their own: ornamenting the façade of hell. If Lichtenberg had found paper money in circulation, the plan of this work would not have escaped him.

Legal Protection for the Needy

Publisher: My expectations have been most rudely disappointed. Your work makes no impression on the public; you do not have the slightest drawing power. And I have spared no expense. I have incurred advertising costs.—You know how highly I think of you, despite all this. But you cannot hold it against me if even I now have to listen to my commercial conscience. If there is anyone who does what he can for authors, I am he. But, after all, I also have a wife and children to look after. I do not mean, of course, that I hold you accountable for the losses of the past years. But a bitter feeling of disappointment will remain. I regret that I am at present absolutely unable to support you further.

Author: Sir, why did you become a publisher? We shall have the answer by return mail. But permit me to say one thing in advance. I figure in your records as number 27. You have published five of my books; in other words, you have put your money five times on number 27. I am sorry that number 27 did not prove a winner. Incidentally, you took only coupled bets. Only because I come next to your lucky number 28.—Now you know why you became a publisher. You might just as well have entered an honest profession, like your esteemed father. But never a thought for the morrow—such is youth. Continue to indulge your habits. But avoid posing as an honest businessman. Don't feign innocence when you've gambled everything away; don't talk about your eight-hour workday, or your nights, when you hardly get any rest. "Truth and fidelity before all else, my child." And don't start making scenes with your numbers! Otherwise you'll be thrown out.

Doctor's Night-Bell

Sexual fulfillment delivers the man from his secret, which does not consist in sexuality but which in its fulfillment, and perhaps in it alone, is severed—not solved. This secret is comparable to the fetters that bind him to life. The woman cuts them, and the man is free to die because his life has lost its secret. Thereby he is reborn, and as his beloved frees him from the mother's spell, the woman literally detaches him from Mother Earth—a midwife who cuts that umbilical cord which is woven of nature's mystery.

Madame Ariane: Second Courtyard on the Left

He who asks fortune-tellers the future unwittingly forfeits an inner intimation of coming events that is a thousand times more exact than anything they may say. He is impelled by inertia, rather than by curiosity, and nothing is more unlike the submissive apathy with which he hears his fate revealed than the alert dexterity with which the man of courage lays hands on the future. For presence of mind is an extract of the future, and precise awareness of the present moment is more decisive than foreknowledge of the most distant events. Omens, presentiments, signals pass day and night through our organism like wave impulses. To interpret them or to use them: that is the question. The two are irreconcilable. Cowardice and apathy counsel the former, lucidity and freedom the latter. For before such prophecy or warning has been mediated by word or image, it has lost its vitality, the power to strike at our center and force us, we scarcely know how, to act accordingly. If we neglect to do so, and only then, the message is deciphered. We read it. But now it is too late. Hence, when you are taken unawares by an outbreak of fire or the news of a death, there is in the first mute shock a feeling of guilt, the indistinct reproach: Were you really unaware of this? Didn't the dead person's name, the last time you uttered it, sound differently in your mouth? Don't you see in the flames a sign from yesterday evening, in a language you only now understand? And if an object dear to you has been lost, wasn't there—hours, days before—an aura of mockery or mourning about it that gave the secret away? Like ultraviolet rays, memory shows to each man in the book of life a script that invisibly and prophetically glosses the text. But it is not with impunity that these intentions are exchanged, that unlived life is handed over to cards, spirits, stars, to be in an instant squandered, misused, and returned to us disfigured; we do not go unpunished for cheating the body of its power to meet the fates on its own ground and triumph. The moment is the Caudine Yoke beneath which fate must bow to the body. To turn the threatening future into a fulfilled "now," the only desirable telepathic miracle, is a work of bodily presence of mind. Primitive epochs, when such demeanor was part of man's daily husbandry, provided him with the most reliable instrument of divination: the naked body. Even the ancients knew of this true practice, and Scipio, stumbling as he set foot on Carthaginian soil, cried out, spreading his arms wide as he fell, the watchword of victory, "Teneo te, terra Africana!"[25] What would have become a portent of disaster he binds bodily to the moment, making himself the fac- totum of his body. In just such mastery, the ancient ascetic exercises of fasting, chastity, and vigil have for all time cel- ebrated their greatest victories. Each morning the day lies like a fresh shirt on our bed; this incomparably fine, incom- parably tightly woven fabric of pure prediction fits us per- fectly. The happiness of the next twenty-four hours depends on our ability, on waking, to pick it up.

Costume Wardrobe

A bearer of news of death appears to himself as very impor- tant. His feeling—even against all reason—makes him a mes- senger from the realm of the dead. For the community of all the dead is so immense that even he who only reports death is aware of it. *Ad plures ire* was the Latins' expression for dying.[26]

At Bellinzona I noticed three priests in the station's waiting room. They were sitting on a bench diagonally op- posite mine. In rapt attention I observed the gestures of the one seated in the middle, who was distinguished from his brothers by a red skullcap. While he speaks to them, his hands are folded in his lap, and only now and then is one or the other very slightly raised and moved. I think to myself: his right hand must always know what the left is doing.

Is there anyone who has not once been stunned, emerging from the Métro into the open air, to step into brilliant sunlight? And yet the sun shone just as brightly a few minutes earlier, when he went down. So quickly has he forgotten the weather of the upper world. And as quickly the world in its turn will forget him. For who can say more of his own existence than that it has passed through the lives of two or three others as gently and closely as the weather?

Again and again, in Shakespeare, in Calderón, battles fill the last act, and kings, princes, attendants, and followers "enter, fleeing." The moment in which they become visible to spectators brings them to a standstill. The flight of the *dramatis personae* is arrested by the stage. Their entry into the visual field of nonparticipating and truly impartial persons allows the harassed to draw breath, bathes them in new air. The appearance on stage of those who enter "fleeing" takes from this its hidden meaning. Our reading of this formula is imbued with expectation of a place, a light, a footlight glare, in which our flight through life may be likewise sheltered in the presence of onlooking strangers.

Betting Office

Bourgeois existence is the regime of private affairs. The more important the nature and implications of a mode of behavior, the further removed it is from observation here. Political conviction, financial situation, religion—all these seek hideouts, and the family is the rotten, dismal edifice in whose closets and crannies the most ignominious instincts are deposited. Mundane life proclaims the total subjugation of eroticism to privacy. So wooing becomes a silent, deadly serious transaction between two persons alone, and this thoroughly private wooing, severed from all responsibility, is what is really new in "flirting." In contrast, the proletarian and the feudal type of man resemble each other in that, in wooing, it is much less the woman than their competitors that they overcome. In this, they respect the woman far more deeply than in her freedom, being at her command without cross-examining her. The shift of erotic emphasis to the public sphere is both feudal and proletarian. To be seen with a woman on such-and-such an occasion can mean more than to sleep with her. Thus, in marriage, too, value does not lie in the sterile "harmony" of the partners: it is as the eccentric offshoot of their struggles and rivalries enacted elsewhere that, like the child, the spiritual force of marriage is manifest.

Stand-Up Beer Hall

Sailors seldom come ashore; service on the high seas is a holiday by comparison with the labor in harbors, where loading and unloading must often be done day and night. When a gang is then given a few hours' shore-leave, it is already dark. At best, the cathedral looms like a dark promontory on the way to the tavern. The ale-house is the key to every town; to know where German beer can be drunk is geography and ethnology enough. The German seamen's bar unrolls the nocturnal map of the city: to find the way from there to the brothel, to the other bars, is not difficult. Their names have criss-crossed the mealtime conversations for days. For when a harbor has been left behind, one sailor after another hoists like little pennants the nicknames of bars and dance-halls, beautiful women and national dishes, from the next harbor. But who knows whether he will go ashore this time? For this reason, no sooner is the ship declared and moored than tradesmen come aboard with souvenirs: chains and picture-postcards, oil-paintings, knives, and marble figurines. The city sights are not seen but bought. In the sailors' chests, the leather belt from Hong Kong is juxtaposed with a panorama of Palermo and a girl's photo from Stettin. And their real habitat is exactly the same. They know nothing of the hazy distances in which, for the bourgeois, foreign lands are enshrouded. What first asserts itself in every city is, first, service on board, and then German beer, English shaving-soap, and Dutch tobacco. Imbued to the marrow with the international norms of industry, they are not the dupes of palms and icebergs. The seaman is sated with proximity, and only the most exact nuances speak to him. He can distinguish countries better by the preparation of their fish than by their building-styles or landscapes. He is so much at home in detail that the ocean routes where he cuts close to other ships (greeting those of his own firm with howls from the ship's horn) become noisy thoroughfares where you have to give way to traffic. He lives on the open sea in a city where, on the Marseilles Cannebière, a Port Said bar stands diagonally opposite a Hamburg brothel, and the Neapolitan Castel dell'Ovo is to be found on Barcelona's Plaza Cataluña. For officers, their native town still holds pride of place. But for the ordinary sailor or the stoker, the people whose transported labor-power maintains contact with the commodities in the hull of the ship, the interlaced harbors are no longer even a homeland, but a cradle. And listening to them, one realizes what mendacity resides in voyaging.

No Vagrants!

All religions have honored the beggar. For he proves that in a matter both as prosaic and holy, banal and regenerating, as the giving of alms, intellect and morality, consistency and principles are miserably inadequate.

We deplore the beggars in the South, forgetting that their persistence in front of our noses is as justified as a scholar's before a difficult text. No shadow of hesitation, no slightest wish or deliberation in our faces escapes their notice. The telepathy of the coachman who, by accosting us, makes known to us our previously unsuspected inclination to board his vehicle, and of the shopkeeper who extracts from his junk the single chain or cameo that could delight us, is of the same order.

To the Planetarium

If one had to expound the teachings of antiquity with utmost brevity while standing on one leg, as did Hillel that of the Jews, it could only be in this sentence:[27] "They alone shall possess the earth who live from the powers of the cosmos." Nothing distinguishes the ancient from the modern man so much as the former's absorption in a cosmic experience scarcely known to later periods. Its waning is marked by the flowering of astronomy at the beginning of the modern age. Kepler, Copernicus, and Tycho Brahe were certainly not driven by scientific impulses alone. All the same, the exclusive emphasis on an optical connection to the universe, to which astronomy very quickly led, contained a portent of what was to come. The ancients' intercourse with the cosmos had been different: the ecstatic trance [*Rausch*]. For it is in this experience alone that we gain certain knowledge of what is nearest to us and what is remotest from us, and never of one without the other. This means, however, that man can be in ecstatic contact with the cosmos only communally. It is the dangerous error of modern men to regard this experience as unimportant and avoidable, and to consign it to the individual as the poetic rapture of starry nights. It is not; its hour strikes again and again, and then neither nations nor generations can escape it, as was made terribly clear by the last war, which was an attempt at new and unprecedented commingling with the cosmic powers. Human multitudes, gases, electrical forces were hurled into the open country, high-frequency currents coursed through the landscape, new constellations rose in the sky, aerial space and ocean depths thundered with propellers, and everywhere sacrificial shafts were dug in Mother Earth. This immense wooing of the cosmos was enacted for the first time on a planetary scale—that is, in the spirit of technology. But because the lust for profit of the ruling class sought satisfaction through it, technology betrayed man and turned the bridal bed into a bloodbath. The mastery of nature (so the imperialists teach) is the purpose of all technology. But who would trust a cane wielder who proclaimed the mastery of children by adults to be the purpose of education? Is not education, above all, the indispensable ordering of the relationship between generations and therefore mastery (if we are to use this term) of that relationship and not of children? And likewise technology is the mastery of not nature but of the relation between nature and man. Men as a species completed their development thousands of years ago; but mankind as a species is just beginning his. In technology, a *physis* is being organized through which mankind's contact with the cosmos takes a new and different form from that which it had in nations and families. One need recall only the experience of velocities by virtue of which mankind is now preparing to embark on incalculable journeys into the interior of time, to encounter there rhythms from which the sick shall draw strength as they did earlier on high mountains or on the shores of southern seas. The "Lunaparks" are a prefiguration of sanatoria.[28] The paroxysm of genuine cosmic experience is not tied to that tiny fragment of nature that we are accustomed to call "Nature." In the nights of annihilation of the last war, the frame of mankind was shaken by a feeling that resembled the bliss of the epileptic. And the revolts that followed it were the first attempt of mankind to bring the new body under its control. The power of the proletariat is the measure of its convalescence. If it is not gripped

to the very marrow by the discipline of this power, no paci-
fist polemics will save it. Living substance conquers the
frenzy of destruction only in the ecstasy of procreation.

Written 1923–1926; published in 1928.
Translated by Edmund Jephcott.

NOTES

1. From the late eighteenth through the early nineteenth century a casino was housed at number 113 in the basement of the Palais Royale in Paris; it was known for gambling and prostitution. For this note and for several others below, the editor is indebted to Detlev Schöttker, the editor of *One-Way Street* in the new German Benjamin edition, *Werke und Nachlaß* (Frankfurt: Suhrkamp Verlag, 2009).

2. Johann Wolfgang von Goethe's house in Weimar had been opened as a museum in 1886.

3. Anna Katherine Green (1846–1935), American detective-story writer, born in Brooklyn, New York. Her thrillers are characterized by logical construction and a knowledge of criminal law. Her most famous book is *The Leavenworth Case* (1878).

4. Gaston Leroux (1868–1927), journalist and author of crime fiction.

5. The Kaiserpanorama opened in the Imperial Arcade (Kaiserpassage) in 1880. It was a round carousel surrounded by twenty-four viewing stations; as the carousel turned, each viewer was presented with a new stereoscopic image.

6. The "German inflation" began as early as 1914, when the imperial government took to financing its war effort with a series of financially disastrous measures. The economic situation was exacerbated in the early years of the Weimar Republic as the fledgling democracy confronted pressing social and political problems, the burden of reparations, and serious inflation. Most references to the inflation, however, intend the hyperinflation of late 1922 and 1923, when the German economy was decimated by one of the worst economic crises to confront a modern industrial state. If we compare late 1913 (the last year before the war) with late 1923 using the wholesale price index as the basis for comparison, we find that one German mark in 1913 equaled 1,261 thousand million marks by December 1923.

7. *Nulla dies sine linea:* "Not a day without a line" (i.e., "without writing a line"). Proverbial expression, from Pliny the Elder, *Natural History* XXXV, 36.

8. Jean Paul Richter (1763–1825) wrote a series of wildly extravagant, highly imaginative novels that combine fantasy and realism.

9. Pharus was the most popular brand of folding city maps in Germany during the 1920s.

10. The quoted lines are from the poem "Tut ein Schilf sich doch hervor." This and "Selige Sehnsucht" are the last poems in Goethe's collection *West-Östlicher Divan* [West-Easterly Divan].

11. Legendary Greek poet of the seventh century BCE. He was cast into the sea by envious sailors, but his lyric song charmed the dolphins, one of which bore him safely to land. The story is told by Herodotus and Plutarch.

12. Benjamin refers to theories of humorism that date from antiquity. Medieval complexion-books represented the ways in which the four human temperaments arise through particular mixtures (complexions) of bodily fluids (humors).

13. Gustav Roethe (1859–1926), professor of German literature at the Friedrich-Wilhelm University in Berlin. Benjamin had studied Old High German with him in 1913/1914.

14. Karl Kraus (1874–1936), Austrian writer and journalist known for his biting satire. Benjamin was an avid reader of Kraus's journal *Die Fackel* (The Torch). Kraus's poem appears in the collection *Worte in Versen* (1920).

15. Atrani is an ancient village in southern Italy, near Naples on the Gulf of Salerno; today it is part of the town of Amalfi. Its church of San Salvatore de Bireto dates from the year 940.

16. The presentation of a fairy story, usually outdoors, using elaborate staging and costumes. Popular in France and England in the seventeenth and eighteenth centuries.

17. André Le Nôtre (1613–1700), French landscape architect. Created the gardens at Versailles and the Jardin des Tuileries, among many others.

18. Boscotrecase is a commune in Napoli province, Campania, about twelve miles southeast of Naples.

19. One of the labors of Hercules involved the cleaning of the stables of the mythical king Augeas, whose cattle herd was the greatest in Greece.

20. An uninhabited island in the Pacific, discovered in 1793 by the Spanish explorer Salas y Gomez. Benjamin no doubt knew the poem of the same name by Adelbert von Chamisso.

21. Humbert (Umberto) I (1844–1900), conservative and pro-German king of Italy (1878–1900), whose portrait graced Italian stamps from 1879 through 1893. Assassinated at Monza, near Milan.

22. Thurn und Taxis: princely house in Germany that was granted the postal concession for the Holy Roman Empire. Synonymous with "mail service" in Europe.

23. Heinrich von Stephan (1831–1897), created the modern German mail system. He was, however, not a contemporary of Jean Paul Richter.

24. Georg Christoph Lichtenberg (1742–1799), satirist and experimental psychologist. Although Lichtenberg was a feared satirist in his time, he is remembered today as the first great German aphorist. More than 1,500 pages of notes were published posthumously; alongside jokes, linguistic paradoxes, puns, metaphors, and excerpts from other writers, they contain thousands of memorable aphorisms.

25. Latin for "I hold you, African earth."

26. Latin for "to go toward the many."

27. Hillel the Elder (ca. 60 BCE–ca. 10 CE), spiritual leader of the Jewish people and the founder of a school of sages.

28. The Luna Park was an amusement park in Halensee at the western end of the Kurfürstendamm in Berlin.

INDEX